# Marketing in the Third World

# Marketing in the Third World

Denise M. Johnson, PhD
Erdener Kaynak, PhD, DSc
Editors

International Business Press
An Imprint of
The Haworth Press, Inc.
New York • London

Published by

International Business Press, 10 Alice Street, Binghamton, NY 13904-1580 USA

International Business Press is an Imprint of the Haworth Press, Inc., 10 Alice Street, Binghamton, NY 13904-1580 USA.

*Marketing in the Third World* has also been published as *Journal of Global Marketing*, Volume 9, Number 4 1996.

The development, preparation, and publication of this work has been undertaken with great care. However, the publisher, employees, editors, and agents of The Haworth Press and all imprints of The Haworth Press, Inc., including The Haworth Medical Press and Pharmaceutical Products Press, are not responsible for any errors contained herein or for consequences that may ensue from use of materials or information contained in this work. Opinions expressed by the author(s) are not necessarily those of The Haworth Press, Inc.

The Haworth Press, Inc., 10 Alice Street, Binghamton, NY 13904-1580 USA

**Library of Congress Cataloging-in-Publication Data**

Marketing in the Third World / Denise M. Johnson, Erdener Kaynak, editors.
     p. cm.
     "Has also been published as Journal of global marketing, volume 9, number 4, 1996"–T.p.verso.
     Includes bibliographical references and index.
     ISBN 1-56024-830-0 (alk. paper)
     1. Export marketing–Developing countries. I. Johnson, Denise M. (Denise Martha), 1953- . II. Kaynak, Erdener.
HF1416.6.D44M37 1996                                96-20073
658.8'48'091724–dc20                                 CIP

# INDEXING & ABSTRACTING

Contributions to this publication are selectively indexed or abstracted in print, electronic, online, or CD-ROM version(s) of the reference tools and information services listed below. This list is current as of the copyright date of this publication. See the end of this section for additional notes.

- *ABI/INFORM Global (broad-coverage indexing & abstracting service that includes numerous English-language titles outside the USA available from University Microfilms International (UMI), 300 North Zeeb Road, P.O. Box 1346, Ann Arbor, MI 48106-1346),* UMI Data Courier, Attn: Library Services, Box 34660, Louisville, KY 40232

- *ABSCAN, Inc.,* P.O. Box 2384, Monroe, LA 71207-2384

- *Business Education Index, The,* Eastern Illinois University, Department of Business Education and Administration Information Systems, Charleston, IL 61920

- *Cabell's Directory of Publishing Opportunities in Business & Economics (conprehensive & descriptive bibliographic listing with editorial criteria and publication production data for selected business & economics journals),* Cabell Publishing Company, Box 5428, Tobe Hahn Station, Beaumont, TX 77726-5428

- *CNPIEC Reference Guide: Chinese National Directory of Foreign Periodicals,* P.O. Box 88, Beijing, People's Republic of China

- *Communication Abstracts,* Temple University, 303 Annenberg Hall, Philadelphia, PA 19122

- *Contents Pages in Management*, University of Manchester Business School, Booth Street West, Manchester M15 6PB, England

- *Foods Adlibra,* Foods Adlibra Publications, 9000 Plymouth Avenue North, Minneapolis, MN 55427

- *Human Resources Abstracts (HRA)*, Sage Publications, Inc., 2455 Teller Road, Newbury Park, CA 91320

(continued)

- *Index to Periodical Articles Related to Law*, University of Texas, 727 East 26th Street, Austin, TX 78705

- *International Political Science Abstracts*, 27 Rue Saint-Guillaume, F-75337 Paris, Cedex 07, France

- *INTERNET ACCESS (& additional networks) Bulletin Board for Libraries ("BUBL"), coverage of information resources on INTERNET, JANET, and other networks.*
  - JANET X.29: UK.AC.BATH.BUBL or 00006012101300
  - TELNET: BUBL.BATH.AC.UK or 138.38.32.45 login 'bubl'
  - Gopher: BUBL.BATH.AC.UK (138.32.32.45). Port 7070
  - World Wide Web: http: / / www.bubl.bath.ac.uk./BUBL/ home.html
  - NISSWAIS: telnetniss.ac.uk (for the NISS gateway)
  The Andersonian Library, Curran Building, 101 St. James Road, Glasgow G4 ONS, Scotland

- *Journal of Health Care Marketing (abstracts section)*, Georgia Tech-School of Management, Ivan Allen College- 225 North Avenue NW, Atlanta, GA 30332

- *Management & Marketing Abstracts*, Pira International, Randalls Road, Leatherhead, Surrey KT22 7RU, England

- *Marketing Executive Report*, American Marketing Association, 250 South Wacker Drive, Chicago, IL 60606

- *Public Affairs Information Bulletin (PAIS)*, Public Affairs Information Service, Inc., 521 West 43rd Street, New York, NY 10036-4396

- *Referativnyi Zhurnal (Abstracts Journal of the Institute of Scientific Information of the Republic of Russia)*, The Institute of Scientific Information, Baltijskaja ul., 14, Moscow A-219, Republic of Russia

- *Sage Public Administration Abstracts (SPAA)*, Sage Publications, Inc., 2455 Teller Road, Newbury Park, CA 91320

- *TOPICATOR*, Topicator, Inc., 205 South Stewart Road #229, Mission, TX 78572-6336

(continued)

# SPECIAL BIBLIOGRAPHIC NOTES

*related to special journal issues (separates)*
*and indexing/abstracting*

☐ indexing/abstracting services in this list will also cover material in any "separate" that is co-published simultaneously with Haworth's special thematic journal issue or DocuSerial. Indexing/abstracting usually covers material at the article/chapter level.

☐ monographic co-editions are intended for either non-subscribers or libraries which intend to purchase a second copy for their circulating collections.

☐ monographic co-editions are reported to all jobbers/wholesalers/approval plans. The source journal is listed as the "series" to assist the prevention of duplicate purchasing in the same manner utilized for books-in-series.

☐ to facilitate user/access services all indexing/abstracting services are encouraged to utilize the co-indexing entry note indicated at the bottom of the first page of each article/chapter/contribution.

☐ this is intended to assist a library user of any reference tool (whether print, electronic, online, or CD-ROM) to locate the monographic version if the library has purchased this version but not a subscription to the source journal.

☐ individual articles/chapters in any Haworth publication are also available through the Haworth Document Delivery Services (HDDS).

# Marketing in the Third World

## CONTENTS

# ABOUT THE EDITORS

**Denise M. Johnson, PhD, Guest Editor,** is currently an Associate Professor and the International Officer in the College of Business and Public Administration at the University of Louisville, Louisville, Kentucky. She received her BS and MBA (Finance) from Michigan State University, East Lansing, Michigan; and her Ph.D. (International Business) from Indiana University, Bloomington, Indiana. Dr. Johnson's current research interests are in the areas of marketing strategies of firms in transitional economies in East Europe and the former Soviet Union; attitudes toward advertising and customer relations in transitional economies; and market education using simulations as learning tools. Dr. Johnson currently serves as a consultant for family businesses in marketing strategy development and implementation, and she has served as a consultant in the banking, health care, automotive, consumer products and sports entertainment industries. She has undertaken research or consulting in 16 countries in North America, South America, Africa, West Europe, East Europe and Asia. Her research has appeared in the *Journal of Global Marketing; Journal of International Marketing; Journal of Strategic Marketing, Journal of Consumer Affairs; Journal of Business Communications; Marketing Education Review; Journal of Marketing Education; Journal of International Consumer Marketing; International Review of Retail, Distribution and Consumer Research;* and *The International Executive*, as well as other academic and practitioner journals.

**Erdener Kaynak, PhD, DSc**, is a Professor of Marketing at the School of Business Administration at The Pennsylvania State University at Harrisburg. He has extensive teaching, research, consulting and advising experience in five continents in over thirty countries. A prolific author, Dr. Kaynak has published 20 books and over 150 articles in refereed scholarly and professional journals on international marketing and cross-national/cultural consumer behavior in a number of languages. One of his books was translated into

Chinese and another one into Japanese. He has served on the Board of Governors of the Academy of Marketing Science and Currently serves in the capacity of Director and Executive Vice-President of International Management Development Association (IMDA). Dr. Kaynak also serves on a dozen or so U.S. and European based marketing and international business journal review boards and is Executive Editor for International Business Press (IBP) as well as being Senior Editor (International Business) for The Haworth Press Inc., where he serves as Editor of *Journal of Global Marketing, Journal of International Consumer Marketing, Journal of Teaching in International Business, Journal of International Food and Agribusiness Marketing, Journal of East-West Business,* and *Journal of Euromarketing.* As a Guest Editor, he has prepared special issues for a number of leading U.S. and European journals. He was also the organizer and Chair or Co-chair of nine major international conferences. Dr. Kaynak is also listed in *Who's Who in America* and *Who's Who in Advertising.*

# Introduction

## Erdener Kaynak

The macroeconomic environment is one of the most important environmental factors contributing to the success or failure of a marketing strategy. There is a stream of research on the effects of stagflation on marketing in a market-oriented developed country, the U.S. (Shama, 1978), on a centrally planned developing country, the old Yugoslavia (Shama, 1992). As centrally planned developing countries move towards market-orientation, it would be useful to further examine different economies along a continuum of orientation as well as economic development to contrast firms' adjustments used in response to stagflation. The article by Roxas and Huszagh relates findings from two of these studies, the Philippines and the U.S. A sample of 142 large Philippine firms were surveyed using a network of personal contracts in targeted firms. Responses were compared with the results of a similar survey of large U.S. firms by Shama (1978) using a z-test for proportions.

Results showed that Philippine firms were more likely to change their product strategy instead of their pricing strategy compared to U.S. firms. This was attributed to reductions in real income due to the recession as well as government response in the form of price controls used in the past involving necessary commodities. Thus, rather than automatic price increases to reflect cost-push inflation, firms are more likely to change the product strategy to cut costs and maintain reasonable profits. Such changes are less perceptible to consumers. Findings from this study can be used as a guide to operating in environments with similar economic constraints. Managers can use the study results to provide insights into effective market development strategies.

[Haworth co-indexing entry note]: "Introduction." Kaynak, Erdener. Co-published simultaneously in the *Journal of Global Marketing* (International Business Press, an imprint of The Haworth Press, Inc.) Vol. 9, No. 4, 1996, pp. 1-4; and: *Marketing in the Third World* (ed: Denise M. Johnson, and Erdener Kaynak) International Business Press, an imprint of The Haworth Press, Inc., 1996, pp. 1-4. Single or multiple copies of this article are available from The Haworth Document Delivery Service [1-800-342-9678, 9:00 a.m. - 5:00 p.m. (EST). E-mail address: getinfo@haworth.com].

The paper by Mercedes Douglas is concerned with investigating the influence of internal and external factors on the performance of Peruvian exporting firms and with expanding existing knowledge on the behavior of exporting firms in developing countries. The diverse environmental variables, particularly the economic and political elements, which determine the external macro environment in Peru were extensively reviewed together with an in-depth review of the extant literature on the micro factors of export performance. The review of the micro factors is the basis for the conceptual framework comprising the various competencies, strategies, and characteristics which influence the success or failure of the various enterprises observed in many countries, particularly of those firms in developed countries.

The determinants of performance in the study were investigated empirically through a postal survey of 25 Peruvian exporters of non-traditional products. The analysis of the sample of small-to-medium sized firms describes their practices and outlines the factors which bear any relevance on the results of the sample as a whole. The field research results indicate that the performance of the firms in the sample is a consequence of the interaction of various factors such as concentration on markets in developed countries, technology, size, management commitment, experience, information of markets abroad and the use of agents and distributors overseas. No associations were found concerning the adaptation of the marketing mix, however this does not imply that these were less important in the perception of the respondents. Financial assistance from the government, although seen as important too, was negatively associated to performance, and only the support of the Peruvian Exporters Association had a positive impact on the firms.

The study by Surjit Chhabra examined the extent of marketing mix adaptations by the American Multinational Corporations in South America for tangible consumer and industrial products. The results indicate that MNC managers should expect to make extensive adaptations in their pricing and promotion elements in this region since a substantial majority of the respondents indicated having to make obligatory adaptations in these two elements of their marketing mix. The top two reasons for adaptations in these elements were cited as market infrastructure and government regulations.

The managers should also investigate the possibility of minimal adaptations in their product elements (to minimize the product development costs) as certain elements of a product offering (e.g., features, ingredients/materials, brand name, etc.) were reported to have much lower levels of adaptation by the respondent MNCs.

Since media coverage of the interior regions of Papua New Guinea is virtually non-existent, an advertising agency has adapted the 'live' theater used in development communications to marketing purposes on behalf of its multinational clients. A drama troupe travels from village to village performing multi-act plays into the scripts of which are woven product information.

In the paper by Amos Owen Thomas, the rugged terrain, cultural diversity and developing economy of the country is described as the backdrop to this advertising practice. As might be expected, professional marketing is embryonic and the mass media offers very limited choices and reach. The mechanics of this medium are then analyzed, i.e., the use of two troupes, the number of locations and types of locations preferred, the criterion for compiling the clients lists, and how the 'live' commercials are crafted, rehearsed and performed. The effectiveness of the medium is also reported and assessed, within the constraints of conducting research in developing countries such as PNG.

The author discusses the politico-economic impact, and ethical implications of *wokabaut* marketing. The claims of the agency to be socially-conscious and culturally-sensitive in their strategy and operations are evaluated and compared with findings in some other developing countries. The paper also points out the sociocultural implications of having an intrusive, dedicated advertising medium in the tribal interior of Papua New Guinea. It concludes with some arguments for greater coordinations of the surrogate marketing activities of multinational corporations with the economic development programmes of such developing countries.

The objective of the paper by Kaynak and Kara is to examine the internationalization process of developing country public-sector enterprises and developing a marketing oriented framework for effective internationalization process. In particular, public sector organizations' entry and operational methods are analyzed in addition to their organizational behavior and strategy formulation while operating in a variety of foreign markets. Public sector organizations show distinct differences in structure, management, philosophy, and performance when compared to private sector organizations. Traditionally, public sector firms were confined to public utilities such as energy, transportation, communications, iron, steel, and coal production and most of their activities were directed to the domestic markets. They are usually autonomously organized with the government providing the initial capital and then monitoring the activities in a constant manner. Over the past several years, pressure for globalization began to develop rapidly and public-sector enterprises now play a more important role in global markets, relative to their domestic operations. It is suggested in this study that the expansion to global markets requires some significant strategy adjustments. In other words, customer orientation for the public sector enterprises means making radical changes in their corporate philosophy. Furthermore, it is expected that developing country public sector enterprises pass through several interconnected dynamic phases in their globalization process. Perhaps government assisted internationalization process could be employed more successfully than other programs. In other words, sequential stages in the globalization process include import substitution, export promotion, and foreign direct investment. It is expected that the effect of the government in the initial stages will be high while it diminishes in the later stages. Future studies should empirically analyze, using secondary and primary data sources, the impact of the globalization on the business operations of the public sector enterprises at domestic markets. This could involve a comparative analysis between the globalized public sector enterprise management/marketing philosophy (i.e., marketing orientation) and domesticated public sector enterprise management/marketing philosophy. Another important area of the study in this subject is the comparison of the marketing strategies of newly globalized public sector enterprises and the marketing strategies of the newly globalized private sector enterprises. It is also desirable to initiate an experimental study to identify the variables and assess their importance in increasing effectiveness of successful public sector enterprises.

The environment under which business is conducted in many developing countries has changed dramatically. The purpose of the article by Sam C. Okoroafo is to determine how marketing activities and performance of foreign and domestic firms have varied in response to the environmental changes.

# Adjusting to Economic Change in Developing Countries: Philippine Firms Cope with Stagflation

Juanita Roxas
Sandra M. Huszagh

**SUMMARY.** To ease the U.S. trade deficit, firms must develop new markets. Third World countries successfully emerging from their Debt Crises of the 1980s are proving to be lucrative markets despite existing stagflation conditions. This study looks at marketers' responses to stagflation in the Philippines. Unlike firms in the U.S., those in the Third World like the Philippines find that price cannot be readily adjusted in response to stagflation. Instead firms tend to modify product strategies to reduce costs and to maintain profitability. Findings from this study can be useful in designing entry strategies

Juanita Roxas is Associate Professor of International Business and Marketing, California State Polytechnic University, is on the graduate faculty and teaches courses in international marketing strategy, marketing research and principles of marketing. Her areas of research include international marketing strategy, applications of marketing to public agencies, direct marketing, and cross-cultural consumer buying behavior in Southern California. Dr. Roxas's recent research has been published in the *International Marketing Review*. Sandra M. Huszagh is Associate Professor of Marketing, University of Georgia, is on the graduate faculty and teaches courses in marketing strategy and international marketing.

The authors would like to thank Dr. Fredrick W. Huszagh, Professor of Law at the University of Georgia School of Law, for insight and expertise which helped guide the conceptualization and implementation of this study.

[Haworth co-indexing entry note]: "Adjusting to Economic Change in Developing Countries: Philippine Firms Cope with Stagflation." Roxas, Juanita, and Sandra M. Huszagh. Co-published simultaneously in the *Journal of Global Marketing* (International Business Press, an imprint of The Haworth Press, Inc.) Vol. 9, No. 4, 1996, pp. 5-34; and: *Marketing in the Third World* (ed: Denise M. Johnson, and Erdener Kaynak) International Business Press, an imprint of The Haworth Press, Inc., 1996, pp. 5-34. Single or multiple copies of this article are available from The Haworth Document Delivery Service [1-800-342-9678, 9:00 a.m. - 5:00 p.m. (EST). E-mail address: getinfo@haworth.com].

*5*

for markets enduring similar economic constraints. *[Article copies available from The Haworth Document Delivery Service: 1-800-342-9678. E-mail address: getinfo@haworth.com]*

## INTRODUCTION

A nation's macroeconomic environment plays a critical role in the success or failure of marketing strategies implemented by firms operating within that environment. In the 1990s, national economies all over the world have demonstrated increased volatility due to a variety of factors like the recessions and wars, catastrophic natural disasters like earthquakes, floods, volcanic eruptions and hurricanes, economic adjustment by eastern European countries, etc. Although these events are not all economic in nature, each of them has had devastating effects on the economies of individual countries involved as well as the world economy.

Economic issues are a fundamental problem for managers trying to lead firms through tough monetary and fiscal times (Douglas and Craig 1995). In particular, the simultaneous occurrence of inflation, shortages and recession can either strengthen a firm's position in the marketplace or limit its options. This phenomenon, labelled stagflation, was first identified in the 1970s and has become more and more common in different areas of the world since that period (Bruno and Sachs 1985).

Firms operating in countries experiencing such economic upheavals must quickly adjust their marketing strategies to respond to these disturbances. Studies in the past examined how large companies responded to these macroeconomic shifts in market-oriented developed countries, notably the U.S. (Kotler, 1974; Shama, 1978). Shama's (1978) study sought to explain the root causes of stagflation in the U.S. during the 1970s and provided a theoretical framework for explaining reactions to stagflation by firms as well as consumers.

In 1992, Shama used his original (1978) questionnaire to measure the impact of stagflation on strategies of firms in the old Yugoslavia and determined how these firms adjusted their marketing mixes in response. He then compared the responses of Yugoslavian managers to those of U.S. managers in the 1978 study. Shama (1992) found that managers in Yugoslavian firms reacted very differently from U.S. managers in response to stagflation. Although Yugoslav managers report the high impact of stagflation on their operations, marketing reaction in the form of changes in the marketing mix was weak. In contrast, U.S. managers reported high impact as well as major strategy changes in response to stagflation. This study showed stark contrasts between "marketing management behavior during stagflation in the planned economy of Yugoslavia with the free market of the USA" (Shama 1992, p. 45).

Shama explained the disparity between the two countries by proposing an alternative framework for marketing activities. The government planner/regulator was central to all marketing activities in Yugoslavia and other centrally planned developing countries in contrast to the consumer focus of all marketing activities in the U.S. (Shama 1992).

During the same year, Huszagh, Roxas and Keck (1992) explored the effects of inflation, shortages and recession on marketing strategies of large manufacturing and non-manufacturing firms in the Philippines. The Philippine study used an instrument patterned after Shama's (1978) but concentrated on and expanded the issues involving the product strategy, pricing strategy, and target market strategy—the top three issues that Shama (1978) found were most heavily impacted in the U.S. Their findings show that although there are differences between firms according to sector, strategies prescribed for U.S. firms during the stagflation years of the 1970s were relevant in the Philippines.

Shama's studies (1978; 1992) show how a difference in paradigms between centrally-planned economies and market-oriented economies results in disparate priorities between managers facing stagflation. Since Yugoslav managers place priority on the needs of the government regulator while U.S. managers focus on the needs of the consumer, reactions to stagflation will therefore be different. In trying to relate the two findings, two major factors stand out highlighting the difference between the Yugoslav and U.S. economies. The first is the degree of government involvement in business. On the one extreme are countries with centrally planned economic systems like the former Eastern block nations and USSR, China, and Cuba with governments that virtually controlled business. The other extreme consists of market-oriented countries like those in Western Europe and the U.S. where markets drove business with relatively minimal government interference. There are points all along this continuum where business and government share market authority, e.g., the U.S. where firms have a great deal of flexibility with relatively minimal government participation, Japan where there is greater government participation in business, and South-east Asian countries including the Philippines where there is more of a partnership between government and private business (Kunio 1985; 1988).

The other major factor that must be considered is degree of economic development. On the one end of this continuum are developed countries like the U.S., Japan, and some Western European countries and on the other end are underdeveloped countries that rely primarily on agriculture to sustain their economies. Yugoslavia, then and today, as well as the Philippines are classified as developing countries somewhere near the center of this continuum while the U.S. is on the developed end (Kunio 1985).

The Philippines is near the middle of both these continua. It has a tradition of market-orientation even before it gained its independence in 1946 from the United States which administered it as an American colony since 1898 (*Business America* 1991; Kunio 1985). The Philippines is classified as a developing country in the continuum of economic development lagging somewhat behind more progressive countries in east Asia and experiencing many fiscal and monetary problems prevalent in Latin America.

Studies that examine individual countries have focused attention on areas of the marketing strategy that are most impacted by stagflation. However, the understanding of this phenomenon will be enhanced by holding up the findings in the Philippines against Shama's (1978) findings in the U.S. in order to provide a frame of reference familiar to many readers. This study examines the extent to which there are commonalities in firms' marketing reactions to stagflation across industry sectors in the two countries. While the instrument used is not exactly the same as Shama's (1978), the issues tested were the ones that Shama found were most heavily impacted by stagflation.

The Philippines experienced extreme stagflation conditions particularly between 1983 and 1986. Along with many developing countries like those in Latin America, the Philippine debt crisis necessitated an agreement with the International Monetary Fund that the government institute austerity measures to stabilize the economy (Aghevli, Kim and Neiss 1987; Bautista 1989; Blejer and Guerrero 1988; *The Economist* September 9, 1990; International Monetary Fund 1985; Huszagh, Huszagh and Roxas 1988; Koch 1989; Miller 1989; Miller 1987; Trinidad 1988). Figure 1 graphically displays the Consumer Price Index reflecting inflation of local prices between 1975 and 1988 as well as growth in the country's Gross National Product in U.S. dollars. This chart demonstrates the presence of stagflation beginning in 1983.

A comprehensive analysis of shortages is beyond is scope of this article. However, published statistics on annual average exchange rates, for example, reveal a doubling of the peso equivalent to the U.S. dollar from P 8.497 in 1982 to P 16.641 by 1984 (National Statistical Coordination Board 1989). Declines were reported in trade, productivity, employment, number of business establishments, and the money supply in the private sector for the same period (National Statistical Coordination Board 1989). In addition, interviews with selected managers in 1988 revealed such desperate shortages in foreign exchange critical for purchase of imported raw materials and supplies that the government relaxed enforcement of foreign exchange restrictions in 1984.

## MARKETING RESPONSES TO ECONOMIC PROBLEMS

Over the years, scholars and practitioners have agreed that the macroeconomic environment plays a vital role in the success or failure of a firm's marketing strategy. Since the 1960s, scholars have called for more research into the relationship between the macroenvironment in general and the macroeconomic environment in particular (Bartels 1968; Boddewyn 1964; Cavusgil and Nevin 1981; Cravens 1974; Jain 1989; Kaynak 1982; Thomas 1974). However, empirical studies on the linkage between the macroeconomic environment and marketing have been sparse (Douglas and Wind 1973/74; Shama 1978; Shama 1981; Shama 1992).

The earliest accounts of the specific links between the macroeconomic environment and marketing were found in the trade literature. A number of articles from the trade press such as "The Squeeze on Product Mix" (*Business Week* January 5, 1974), "Pricing Strategy in an Inflation Economy" (*Business Week* April 6, 1974), "The Two-Way Squeeze on New Products" (*Business Week* August 10, 1974) and "Marketing When the Growth Slows" (*Business Week* April 14, 1975) were frequently cited in scholarly studies dealing with marketing mix changes implemented by U.S. manufacturing companies during the period 1974-1975 (Cullwick 1975; Hanna, Kisilbash, and Smart 1975; Kotler 1974; Shama 1978; Shuptrine and Osmanski 1975). Articles published in scholarly journals during the period contained accounts of the effects of the oil crisis which plunged the U.S. economy into stagflation. These studies included prescriptions for changing firms' marketing strategies in response to this combination of inflation, recession, and shortages (Cravens 1974; Cullwick 1975; Kelley and Scheewe 1975; King and Cleland 1974; Kotler 1973; Kotler 1974; Shuptrine and Osmanski 1975; Thomas 1974).

Reflecting the academic and trade literature of the period, Shama (1978) surveyed large U.S. companies to measure the impact of stagflation on marketing. His instrument consisted of questions investigating the adjustments made by firms in their marketing strategies. Shama's study provided three major contributions to the field of marketing. First, it provided empirical evidence linking the economic environment to company marketing activities. Second, his data revealed which element of the marketing mix was most vulnerable to economic changes. And finally, Shama's study provided empirical support for many of the prescriptions pro-

FIGURE 1. Philippine Stagflation Indicators

Inflation and GNP Growth, 1975-1988 (%)

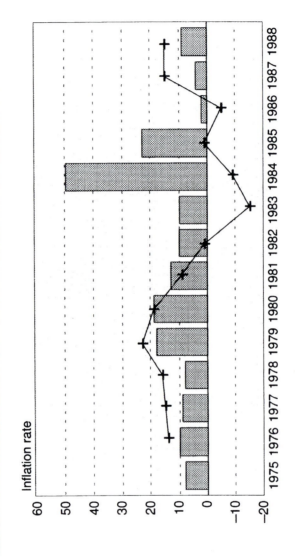

Source: *Philippine Statistical Yearbook, 1989.*

vided in contemporary literature regarding marketing mix changes which effectively cope with stagflation.

## RESEARCH OBJECTIVES

Huszagh, Roxas, and Keck (1992) used the Shama (1978) findings as a springboard to examine differences in responses to stagflation by two industry sectors in a Third World market, the Philippines. One of the objectives of this and the current study is to determine whether marketing strategies designed in a developed country like the U.S. can be applied to Third World markets. This objective carries precedent value in the work of Akaah, Dadzie, and Riordan (1988) whose findings suggest that marketing concepts and management activities designed in developed countries like the U.S. are indeed applicable to Third World countries under specific conditions. The Philippines provides a logical choice because of its history of close economic ties with the U.S.–first as a U.S. colony (1898-1935), then a U.S. Commonwealth (1935-1946) (Kunio 1985). A second objective is to further probe the effects of stagflation on Philippine firms.

Overall results of the Huszagh, Roxas, and Keck (1992) study demonstrated that firms in the Philippines respond quite similarly to firms in the U.S. under stagflation effects, but that there are differences between sectors–with manufacturing firms much more sensitive to stagflation compared to services firms. Given such sector-specific sensitivities, the value added by this research is to compare the effects of stagflation on specific marketing mix elements across both sectors. Since Shama (1978) found that the effects on the marketing mix were unequal, this study tests whether changes reported by Philippine managers were similar to those of U.S. managers. Comparisons between U.S. and Philippine firms will be limited to specific issues included by Shama (1978) in his study relating to the product, price, and target market strategy. Promotion and distribution, while vital to the success of an overall marketing strategy, are the two elements of the marketing mix most difficult to standardize across countries (Huszagh, Fox, and Day 1985). In addition, qualitative research involving long interviews of Philippine managers during the exploratory phase of this study revealed minimal variation in responses to questions dealing with either promotion or distribution. Therefore, no hypotheses were tested for these mix areas.

Thus, we propose parsimonious concentration on the areas of the marketing strategy most heavily influenced by the economic environment. The following mix elements were isolated and tested to assess whether firms in the Philippines were similarly affected by inflation, shortages and recession as U.S. firms were in Shama's (1978) study:

> *Pricing strategy:* Firms face a problem of rising costs while trying to maintain an acceptable profit margin in a recessionary environment (Kotler 1974; Madigan, Miles, Hamilton, and Levine 1989). The responses by firms in Shama's (1978) study showed the most pronounced adjustments made by 98 percent of his sample were frequent price increases closely followed by a greater emphasis on profit margin reported by 66 percent. It was therefore recommended that strategies include frequent adjustment of prices (upward), changing price differentials to influence demand, tightening credit, centralizing price decisions, dropping marginal accounts, and whenever possible, treating customers selectively to maximize loyalty. (Kotler 1974; Hanna, Kizilbash, and Smart 1975; Shama 1978)

During the time of Shama's (1978) study, U.S. inflation rates fluctuated from a low rate of 3.3 percent in 1972 to highs of 11 percent in 1974 and 9.9 percent in 1975. It was estimated that in 1979 the rate would reach 13 percent (Shama 1980). Although the actual inflation rate for 1979 did not reach double digit levels, studies on managers' and consumers' reaction must take this expectation into consideration. Inflation rates between the Philippines (Figure 1) and the U.S. are significantly different. However, U.S. firms and consumers experienced price shocks when inflation rates doubled and almost tripled during the period, since they were used to inflation rates well below 5 percent prior to 1970 (Bruno and Sachs 1985). Likewise, Philippine consumers and managers experienced massive fluctuations in inflation. Inflation rates doubled and more than tripled from the 8 to 12 percent in prior years to 50.3 percent in 1984 and 23.1 percent in 1985 (National Statistical Coordination Board 1989).

Therefore, in order to ensure that respondents had a common reference point for survey questions relating to inflation, we obtained a copy of the *Philippine Statistical Yearbook, 1989*, published by the National Statistical Coordination Board. This source contained annual inflation rates for the period 1973-1988. Averaging all complete annual rates yielded 14.99 percent. When we averaged only the rates between 1981 and 1988, the resulting average inflation rate was 15.03 percent. Thus, the 15 percent rate used in the survey was historically derived. This leads to the following hypothesis:

> H1:  Marketers in the Philippines responded to inflation by adjustments similar to those in the U.S. by focusing more attention

on the pricing strategy (i.e., raising prices to reflect inflation and maintain profits).

To test this hypothesis, respondents were first asked a general question dealing with how much a 15 percent inflation rate affects their pricing strategies overall. Managerial responses will next be compared to responses of U.S. managers in Shama's (1978) study. Additional questions were designed to measure specific pricing strategies recommended by Shama (1978) and prescribed in the literature, i.e., whether prices are adjusted periodically upward to keep up with costs, price differentials among products are changed to emphasize profits, pricing decisions were centralized by tightening credit, and extra services were provided to justify higher prices.

> *Product strategy:* The product strategy has become critical in recent years since large business-to-business customers are reportedly resisting price increases (Schiller 1989). Numerous prescriptions have been provided in the scholarly literature for changes in the product strategy, for instance, Kotler (1974) recommended intense market research, increased segmentation, and product redesign focusing on functionality and economy, and Hanna, Kizilbash, and Smart (1975) encouraged product modifications through downgrading and developing new products that either use less material or less energy.

The trade press reports that businesses' typical responses to inflation, recession and shortages are re-engineering or proactively managing production through product elimination or cost-cutting measures such as closing plants, changing designs and modifying styles (*Business Week* January 9, 1989; Stewart 1990; Treece and Zellner 1989). These adjustments reflect some of the earlier prescriptions for stagflation such as pruning the product line and reallocating resources to the most productive areas (Kotler 1974), narrowing the product line (Hanna, Kizilbash, and Smart 1975), refocusing attention on product quality, product elimination, and diversification decisions (Cullwick 1975), and dropping products with lower margins in favor of higher margin, specialty products (*Business Week* January 5, 1974). Shama (1978) found that among some 33 percent of his sample product elimination was related to stagflation.

A corollary to this issue is research and development. In order to implement changes in the product strategy, research and development activities are requisite to determine the changes required. The literature advocates product redesign to find new ways of serving unmet needs, developing substitutes for products or raw materials, and exploring alternative production or processing methods to stretch existing materials (Cullwick 1975; Hanna, Kizilbash, and Smart 1975; Kotler 1974; Stewart 1990). Although only 25 percent of firms in Shama's (1978) study reported significant effects on research and development activities, he recommends the use of less expensive or lower-quality materials, introduction of substitute products and innovation. Thus, the following hypothesis is examined:

> H2: During stagflation Philippine marketers will respond to shortages in raw materials and supplies in a manner similar to U.S. marketers by changing their product strategy.

To test this hypothesis, we compare responses from Philippine and U.S. managers when asked about the magnitude of changes in their product lines. Then, specific questions will deal with issues like whether shortages result in narrowings of product lines and whether companies engage substantially in research and development activities to alter the product strategy and/or find substitute raw materials.

> *Target Market:* Changes in the macroeconomic environment will change customer preferences (Shama 1978). Literature from the 1970s previewed marketing responses ranging from demarketing, allocating products among customers on a preferential basis, to selling only to profitable customers. (Cravens 1974; Hanna, Kizilbash, and Smart 1975; Kotler 1974)

Although emphasized in the literature, only 24 percent of Shama's (1978) respondents increased consumer research and a mere 12 percent reported that they capitalized on new markets. Literature during the 1980s has shifted strategic focus to the global marketplace. Holstein and Bremner (1989) report on the growth of markets in Asia, Europe, and Canada. Currently Latin America, Asia, and Eastern Europe are areas of the world that marketers are seriously examining (Belli 1991; Goodman and Loveman 1991; Martinez, Quelch, and Ganitsky 1992).

In keeping with the original study by Shama (1978), however, only the following hypothesis is tested:

> H3: There will be a similarity between U.S. and Philippine marketers' responses with regards to changes in strategies towards the target market by adjusting their treatment of the target market.

To test this hypothesis responses were compared between U.S. and Philippine managers on questions relating to the following issues:

- changes in customer services
- the degree to which firms avoided marginal accounts
- whether companies will renew their search for and focus on selling to profitable customers
- whether firms continue to carry marginally profitable products
- the extent to which firms vigorously target new markets

## METHODOLOGY

### Instrument

The questionnaire used in our study consisted of a combination of structured multiple choice questions and itemized rating scales designed to examine managerial responses to inflation, shortages, and recession (see Appendix A). This instrument also included questions regarding the degree to which each element of the marketing mix was affected. Questions were patterned after the Shama (1978) study but were modified to add details and increase clarity.

Survey questions were formulated using exploratory research conducted in three stages. First, issues were pre-tested using "Cultural Insiders" (Converse and Presser 1986). In this phase, a small sample of 13 marketing managers in the Philippines were interviewed using open-ended questions that were administered through personal interviews lasting at least 1.5 hours. This exercise served to establish that: (1) English should be used as the language for the instrument and (2) marketing terms to be used in the instrument were similarly defined and understood by respondents.

The second phase in the design of the instrument consisted of pretesting the modified Shama (1978) questionnaire using "Professional Experts" (Converse and Presser 1986). For this stage, five faculty members from the University of Georgia Department of Marketing and Distribution and School of Law who were conversant with international marketing and macroeconomic issues were asked to critique the instrument. Finally, the standard pretest was conducted using three Filipino executives who were visiting the U.S. and were representative of the respondents in the Philippines. The pretest highlighted the need for modifying the questionnaire to ensure that respondents fully understood each question and used the same frame of reference.

Response rates are crucial to studies of this kind. Since the survey was to be sent overseas, all standard strategies were used to increase response rates. One major concern was questionnaire length. Although Kanuk and

Berenson (1975) report that tests regarding the effects of questionnaire length on response rates yielded no significant results, a rule of thumb in marketing research states that mail questionnaires should not exceed six pages in length (Zikmund 1991). A full replication of Shama's (1978) study would have resulted in an instrument much longer than six pages. Therefore, it became necessary to shorten our instrument to include only the most significant areas, namely, price, product and target market and to forego the areas of promotion and distribution.

### Sample and Administration

The Philippines was chosen as the site for the survey because its economy had experienced a combination of inflation, shortages, and recession as recently as 1983, and appeared to be on the brink of this phenomenon again in 1988. This was also the Third World country in the Pacific Rim where we could find local contacts to facilitate responses. By the time the survey was administered, a new economic upheaval triggered by the Gulf crisis of August 1990 plunged the country once more into a round of inflation, shortages and recession, thus strengthening the validity of the findings in this study (Huszagh, Roxas and Keck 1992).

The list of the *Best 1000 Corporations in the Philippines* (Mahal Kong Pilipinas Foundation, 1989) was the sample frame. This list is the equivalent of the *Fortune 500*, the population in Shama's study. The computer software *Minitab* was used to generate 456 random numbers between 1 and 1000. These numbers were matched with the numerical rankings of firms from the list of the *Best 1000* and the resulting 456 corporations were the target for the surveys.

Surveys were addressed to Marketing Vice Presidents, Marketing Directors or Chief Operating Officers of the corporations. The instrument was sent via air cargo to one author's family member in the Philippines who was provided with a list of targeted corporate executives. This local liaison solicited commitments from family members, friends, coworkers, and business contacts to use their respective networks to reach appropriate executives in as many of the targeted firms as possible. These personal contacts were asked to intercede and facilitate response (Douglas and Craig 1983). Surveys were hand-delivered by these contacts. Survey forms were also mailed out to firms either located outside the Greater Manila Area or where no contacts could be identified. Follow-ups were conducted by phone or mail. Usable responses came from 142 firms located throughout the country, although a large majority of these firms were headquartered in the Greater Manila Area.

## ANALYSIS OF FINDINGS

Comparisons between U.S. and Philippine firms will be limited to specific issues treated by Shama (1978) relating to the product, price, and target market strategy. This analysis compares responses in the top two categories for those questions which dealt with magnitude of impact on these areas.

*Comparisons of Element Strategies:* Figure 2 plots the proportion of respondents who answered in the top two categories for questions dealing with the impact of stagflation on price, product and target market strategies respectively. A significantly lower proportion of Philippine managers reported substantial impact on pricing strategies as a result of stagflation compared to U.S. managers. On the other hand, a larger proportion of Philippine managers reported that the product strategy was substantially affected by stagflation compared to U.S. managers.

Table 1 details the comparison between U.S. (Shama 1978) and Philippine managers' perceptions of the impact of inflation, shortages, and recession on pricing strategies, product line strategies, and target market strategies, respectively. Significant differences were found between the two studies in the effects on prices, changes in product line, and product elimination. On the other hand, there were marked similarities in responses to questions dealing with impact on credit decisions, changes in research and development, and changes in customer service.

*Pricing strategy.* In the area of pricing, the table shows that more than half of all firms in both countries reported frequent price increases. However, the proportion of Philippine firms raising prices at rates equal to or above inflation is significantly less than the proportion of U.S. firms that report frequent price increases.

Differences between U.S. and Philippine firms may be attributed to two major issues of concern during the time that measurements were taken. First, some Philippine managers interviewed in 1988 reported that their firms had recently faced the threat of government price controls particularly for products classified as necessary commodities. This parallels conditions faced by U.S. firms in 1971 with mandatory wage and price controls started on August 15, 1971 and slowly dismantled by early 1974 (Blinder 1979). Philippine managers took the threats seriously and held back on frequent price changes while U.S. firms did not. This difference in reaction reflects the degree of government involvement in business. Philippine firms experience the effects of government action directly unlike U.S. firms. The second issue was the timing of survey administration which was during the Gulf Crisis which again resulted in inflation and recession causing real incomes to decrease.

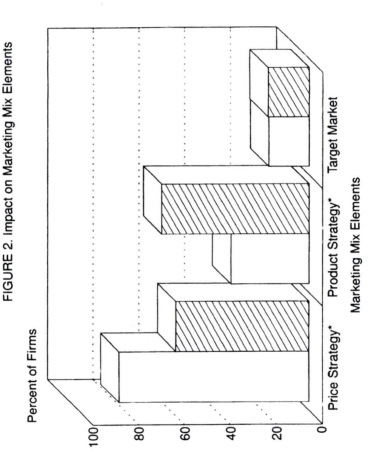

FIGURE 2. Impact on Marketing Mix Elements

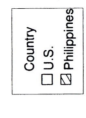

Country
☐ U.S.
▨ Philippines

* Difference significant at alpha = .01

18

## TABLE 1. Product Strategy Changes

| ADJUSTMENTS TO STRATEGY | U.S. (%) | PHILIPPINES (%) |
|---|---|---|
| **PRICING STRATEGY** | | |
| Effects on selling prices | 82.7 | 57.7** |
| -Frequent price adjustment | 98.1[a] | 76.9[b]** |
| -Stronger emphasis on profit margin | 62.5 | 20.4** |
| -Competitive pricing | 36.5 | 19.0** |
| -Extra services to justify higher price | 9.6 | 50.7** |
| Effects on credit decisions | 37.5 | 36.6 |
| -Stricter credit | 58.6 | 73.9* |
| **PRODUCT LINE STRATEGY** | | |
| Changes in product line | 33.7 | 64.0** |
| -Product line reduction | 38.5 | 7.7** |
| Product elimination | 32.7 | 7.7** |
| Changes in research and development | 25.0 | 35.2 |
| -Increased R & D | 38.4 | 14.4** |
| -Develop alternative raw materials | 34.6 | 46.5 |
| **TARGET MARKET STRATEGY** | | |
| Changes in customer service | 17.3 | 17.6 |
| -Avoid marginal accounts | 54.8 | 41.6* |
| -Better servicing of faithful accounts | 50.0 | 59.8 |
| -Consumer research | 24.1 | 57.1** |
| -Carry marginal products | 21.1 | 38.6** |
| -Find new markets | 11.6 | 67.6** |

[a] Includes all positive responses
[b] All responses indicating raising prices at or higher than inflation rate

* Differences are significant at $\alpha = .05$
** Differences are significant at $\alpha = .01$

There were significantly more Philippine firms who tightened credit while significantly less of them engaged in competitive pricing. In the absence of a reliable, accurate and centralized credit reporting system, credit in the Philippines is provided based on findings in formal credit checks as well as endorsements of owners' and/or managers' characters provided by trusted peers (Paine 1992). During an economic crisis, working capital requirements force firms to allocate available credit only to very important customers.

*Product Strategy.* Table 1 presents details of the comparison between firms' responses to questions dealing with changes in the product strategy. The proportion of Philippine managers reporting changes in the product line were almost twice as large as U.S. managers. On the other hand, the table also shows that far fewer Philippine firms reduced their product line compared to U.S. firms. Changes in research and development activities between the two countries were not significantly different. They involved finding alternative raw materials as well as substitute products.

In an effort to examine changes more closely, the Philippine instrument included such issues as whether new products were introduced during the period and the type of new products introduced, types of products eliminated and reasons for these eliminations, issues concerning inventory control directly affecting the product strategy, and directions taken for research and development efforts. Changes in the product strategy were made largely in the area of new product development where close to 50 percent of firms reported introduction of new products. A majority of these new products were either similar to existing lines (according to 48 percent of the sample) or cheaper, more functional products (reported by 33 of the sample). Of the firms who eliminated products, the main reason cited was shortage of raw materials/supplies. Changes in inventory control consisted largely of stockpiling (cited by 73 percent), and shifts in research and development consisted of researching substitute raw materials (mentioned by 49 percent). However, since these specific issues were not included in Shama's (1978) instrument, no comparisons to U.S. responses were possible.

*Target Market/Consumers.* The final section of Table 1 compares responses of U.S. firms and Philippine firms on issues regarding the target market strategy. A similar proportion of firms in both countries report better servicing of faithful accounts. However, a far higher proportion of Philippine firms report that they are searching for and exploiting new markets, notably the export market. This is another artifact of differences between the two countries in economic conditions as well as the bargaining power of firms at the time measurements were taken. During the

1970s, U.S. businesses emphasized the domestic market. As a result, inroads were made by many foreign manufacturers in automobiles, steel, and electronics which seemed of minimal concern to U.S. managers at that time. On the other hand, the size of the Philippine economy is but a fraction of that of the U.S. It has traditionally depended on export earnings to supplement domestic GNP and is aggressively diversifying its economy to shift from exports of commodities to finished goods.

## CONCLUSION

Table 2 compares strategies and tactics prescribed for U.S. firms facing stagflation as summarized by Shama (1978) to those used by Philippine firms faced with similar economic conditions. The table shows that many of the same strategies and tactics were found to be applicable in both environments. The most striking difference involves pricing. Philippine firms were much more conservative in changing prices compared to U.S. firms. For goods and services consumed domestically, this restraint could be explained by the threat of government action in the form of price controls, as well as the decrease in real income in a country where a low percentage of the population can be considered middle class. Thus, to preserve purchasing power, firms must emphasize changes that are less perceptible to consumers but maintain profitability–the product strategy. This is borne out by research and development activities reported which focused primarily on finding substitute materials as well as substitute product offerings to lower costs and preserve profit margins.

Exported goods and services, on the other hand, are faced with a complex set of factors found in global competition. In most instances, Philippine marketers do not have sufficient bargaining power to prescribe terms for international transactions. The pricing strategy is particularly vulnerable to macroenvironmental conditions surrounding each product. Thus, Philippine marketers competing in a global market face conditions such as: (1) government action in the Philippines geared towards encouraging exports in some product categories while taxing cash cow exports in others (International Monetary Fund 1986), (2) tariff and non-tariff barriers erected by importing nations, and most importantly, (3) the forces of competition, among supplier and buyer economies where prices are set by the world market, especially for commodities. Philippine marketers lack bargaining power in this arena to successfully depart from the dollar prices for goods and services set by these external forces. Therefore, managers interviewed in 1988 during the preliminary stage of this study reported

TABLE 2. Comparison Between Adaptive Strategies/Tactics in U.S. and Those in the Philippines

| Strategy/Tactics Prescribed in U.S.: | | | Strategies/Tactics Used in Philippines: |
|---|---|---|---|
| Shortage | Inflation | Recession | Stagflation |
| Product:<br>1. Narrow product line<br>2. Offer cheaper, more functional products<br>3. Purchase shortage raw materials carefully<br>4. Make shortage material go further<br>5. Invest in researching substitute materials<br>6. Introduce substitute products<br>7. Avoid quantity discounts<br><br>Price:<br>1. Raise prices<br>2. Adjust prices periodically (upward)<br>3. Change price differential among products to change demand<br>4. Stop discounts<br>5. Tighten credit<br>6. Centralize price decisions<br><br>Consumers:<br>1. Study effects on consumers<br>2. Drop marginal accounts<br>3. Selective treatment of consumers | Product:<br>1. Narrow product line<br>2. Offer cheaper, more functional products<br>3. Purchase shortage raw materials carefully<br>4. Use less expensive (or lower grade) material in production<br>5. Invest in researching substitute materials<br>6. Avoid quantity discounts<br><br>Price:<br>1. Raise prices<br>2. Adjust prices frequently (upward)<br>3. Change price differential among products to change demand<br>4. Stop discounts<br>5. Tighten credit<br>6. Centralize price decisions<br><br>Consumers:<br>1. Study effects on consumers<br>2. Drop marginal accounts<br>3. Selective treatment of consumers | Product:<br>1. Narrow product line<br>2. Offer cheaper, more functional products<br>3. Cut top of product line<br>4. Use less raw materials in production<br>5. Offer quantity discounts<br><br>Price:<br>1. Lower prices<br>2. Change price differential among products to change demand<br>3. Offer discounts<br>4. Loosen credit<br>5. Centralize price decisions<br><br>Consumers:<br>1. Study effects on consumers<br>2. Cultivate marginal accounts<br>3. Selective treatment of consumers | Product:<br>1. Narrow product line<br>2. Offer cheaper, more functional products<br>3. Stockpile shortage raw materials<br>4. Use cheaper/less raw material for production<br>5. Invest in researching substitute materials<br><br>Price:<br>1. Stabilize prices<br>2. Adjust prices gradually (upward)<br>3. Change price differential among products to change demand<br>4. No change in discounts<br>5. Centralize price decisions<br><br>Consumers:<br>1. Study effects on consumers<br>2. Keep marginal accounts<br>3. Selective treatment of consumers |

that they must compensate for this lack of control over prices by implementing changes in the product strategy.

Other explanatory variables are the degree to which the population–managers and customers alike–have been sensitized to inflation by its frequency in the past, their previous responses to its occurrence, and government action as a result of stagflation in previous years. Elite interviews in 1988 also revealed that drastic reductions in sales volume resulting from price increases during past inflationary periods had resulted in more conservative management attitudes towards passing on cost increases to consumers. Managers interviewed mentioned that radical price increases in response to cost-push inflation had triggered government-imposed price controls on basic commodities in the past. Both decreased sales and government intervention have contributed to a more cautious approach to pricing.

Scholarly literature in marketing has highlighted the importance of the economic environment to marketing success (Cundiff and Hilger 1979; Duhaime, McTavish, and Ross 1985), although the lack of empirical studies examining this relationship is evident. This study confirms the vital role played by the economic environment. In addition, our study provides empirical support for the linkage between the macroeconomic environment and marketing strategies. Finally, the study submits additional evidence that marketing principles first implemented in the U.S. are indeed applicable in other environments, when macroeconomic conditions are similar. Although response frequencies between the two countries were significantly different for many issues, it is important to note that Philippine managers found U.S. marketing procedures relevant to the context of their operations when faced with stagflation-like conditions and responded accordingly.

In an era of globalization where firms in larger numbers are attempting to expand markets internationally as well as domestically, the need for guidance in navigating often perilous waters in new markets has become critical. Companies marketing overseas have traditionally been larger firms which have achieved varying degrees of success. For the 1990s, international markets will be expanded primarily by small and medium sized firms (Holstein 1989; Stewart 1990). With guidance on the appropriate marketing strategies, such firms can be encouraged to enter those more progressive Third Word countries which have recovered from the debt crisis of the 1980s and are now proving to be lucrative markets. The economic environment will always be a major factor for marketers given its impact on demand and profitability. Given such prominence, the guidelines developed from this study can be empirically tested in markets with common bonds throughout the Third World.

## LIMITATIONS OF THE STUDY

In the course of implementing this study, we identified several areas of concern. First, our research was not an exact replication of Shama's work since the questions and scales were expanded and modified for clarity. Additional questions were included to determine specific tactical changes implemented as a result of stagflation. However, since Shama's (1978) original instrument did not contain equivalent questions, comparisons could not be presented for these additional questions. The Philippine questionnaire is provided in Appendix A to show readers exactly how information reported in the findings were derived.

Second, was the issue of possible interactive effects between the political and the economic environment. This study does not purport to isolate variables that are a part of the political environment from variables in the economic environment. Furthermore, preliminary interviews conducted in the Philippines in 1988 indicated that businesspersons attributed adjustments to their marketing strategies primarily to changes in the economic environment. During the course of these interviews, political factors were alluded to only when prompted by the interviewer. It was clear that managers were mainly concerned about the economic environment.

Third, we recognize the problems of comparing two very disparate economies like the U.S and the Philippines. While we acknowledge problems in comparing managerial actions across these two countries, merely presenting the results of the Philippine study will not be quite so meaningful without a broader context that the comparison provides. Anticipating that a majority of readers will use the U.S. as a frame of reference, we tried to establish similarities in macroeconomic conditions to enable readers to evaluate the merits of these findings themselves.

Fourth, the survey was designed and written after it was established that the Philippines had indeed experienced stagflation. Since we could not predict when the next period of stagflation would occur, survey questions were written as hypothetical questions and thus required a common frame of reference between respondents. We therefore included a reference rate of 15 percent which was derived historically. Just as the surveys were finally sent to Manila, the Gulf Crisis occurred causing another foreign exchange crisis and driving up inflation (Huszagh, Roxas and Keck 1992). We feel this strengthened our findings since managers were responding to our questions based on current practices.

Finally, it is unfortunate that the instrument was not designed to accommodate complex statistical analyses which would provide the basis for modeling techniques. This study was designed to examine one section of Shama's (1978) framework dealing with adjustments made by marketing managers to the phenomenon of stagflation and only in the areas of pricing, product and the target market. The areas of promotion and distribution remain viable topics for future stagflation research. This study can also provide the basis for exploring managerial reaction to stagflation in countries located in other parts of the continua.

## REFERENCES

Akaah, Ishmael P., Kofi Q. Dadzie, and Edward A. Riordan (1988), "Applicability of Marketing Concepts and Management Activities in the Third World: An Empirical Investigation," *Journal of Business Research*, vol. 16, no. 2, pp. 133-148.

Bartels, Robert (1968), "Are Domestic and International Marketing Dissimilar?" *Journal of Marketing*, (July) 56-61.

Bautista, Romeo M. (1989), *Impediments to Trade Liberalization in the Philippines*, Aldershot, Hampshire, U.K.: Gower for the Trade Policy Research Center, London.

Belli, Pedro (1991), "Globalizing the Rest of the World," *Harvard Business Review*, (July-August) 50-55.

Blejer, Mario I. and Isabel Guerrero (1988), "Stabilization Policies and Income Distribution in the Philippines," *Finance and Development*, December, pp. 6-8.

Blinder, Alan S. *Economic Policy and the Great Stagflation*, Academic Press: New York, 1979.

Boddewyn, Jean (1964), *Comparative Management and Marketing*, New York: Scott, Foresman.

Bruno, Michael and Jeffrey D. Sachs (1985). *Economics of Worldwide Stagflation*, Harvard University Press: Cambridge, MA.

*Business America* (1991), "Philippines Enacts Liberal Investment Law," (September 9), pp. 11-12.

*Business Week* (1974), "The Squeeze on Product Mix," (January 5), pp. 50-55.

*Business Week* (1974), "Pricing Strategy in an Inflation Economy," (April 6), pp. 43-49.

*Business Week* (1974), "The Two-way Squeeze on New Products," (August 10), pp. 130-132.

*Business Week* (1975), "Marketing When the Growth Slows," (April 14), pp. 45-50.

*Business Week* (1989), "Four Companies Prepare for the Promise—and Perils—of 1989," (January 9), pp. 66-67.

Cavanagh, Jonathan (1988), "Peru Sets Austerity to Fight Inflation and Buoy Reserves," *Wall Street Journal*, (March 7), 17.

Cavusgil, S. Tamer and John R. Nevin (1981), "The State of the Art in International Marketing: An Assessment," *Review of Marketing: 1981*, American Marketing Association.

Converse, Jean M. and Stanley Presser (1986) *Survey Questions: Handcrafting the Standardized Questionnaire*. Sage University Paper series on Quantitative Applications in the Social Sciences, 07-063. Beverly Hills: Sage Publications.

Cravens, David W. (1974), "Marketing Management in an Era of Shortages," *Business Horizons*, (February) 79-85.

Cullwick, David (1975), "Positioning Demarketing Strategy," *Journal of Marketing*, (April), 51-57.

Cundiff, Edward and Marye Tharp Hilger (1979), "Marketing and the Production-Consumption Thesis in Economic Development," in *Macromarketing: Evolution of Thought*, George Fisk, Robert W. Nason, and Phillip D. White, eds., Boulder: Business Research Division, Graduate School of Business Administration, University of Colorado.

Douglas, Susan P. and C. Samuel Craig (1995), *Global Marketing Strategy*, McGraw-Hill: New York.

____ (1983), *International Marketing Research*, Prentice-Hall: Englewood Cliffs, New Jersey.

____ and Yoram Wind (1973-74), "Environmental Factors and Marketing Practices," *European Journal of Marketing*, 7, No. 3, 155-165.

Duhaime, Carole P., Ronald McTavish, and Christopher A. Ross (1985), "Social Marketing: An Approach to Third-World Development," *Journal of Macromarketing*, (Spring), pp. 3-13.

*The Economist* (1990), "Philippines: Pray for It," September 9, p. 29-30.

Goodman, John B. and Gary W. Loveman (1991), "Does Privatization Serve the Public Interest," *Harvard Business Review*, (November-December), pp. 28-38.

Hanna, Nessim, A.H. Kisilbash and Albert Smart (1975), "Marketing Strategy Under Conditions of Economic Scarcity," *Journal of Marketing*, (January) 63-80.

Holstein, William J. and Brian Bremner (1989), "The Little Guys are Making it Big Overseas," *Business Week*, February 27, pp. 94-96.

Huszagh, Sandra M., Juanita P. Roxas and Kay L. Keck (1992), "Marketing Practices in the Changing Philippine Macroeconomic Environment," *International Marketing Review*, vol. 9, no. 1 1992, 32-43.

____, Richard J. Fox, and Ellen Day (1985), "Global Marketing: An Empirical Investigation," *Columbia Journal of World Business*, (20th Anniversary Issue), pp. 31-43.

____, Fredrick W. Huszagh, and Juanita Roxas (1988), "Relationship Between IMF Austerity and Business Marketing Practices in Developing Countries," published in the *Proceedings of the Second International Conference on Marketing and Development*, in Budapest, July, 1988.

International Monetary Fund (1985), "New Fund Study Reviews Debt Restructurings, Notes That Basic Approach Remains Unchanged," *IMF Survey*, (November 25), 359-361.

Jain, Subhash C. (1989), "Standardization of International Marketing Strategy: Some Research Hypotheses," *Journal of Marketing*, (January), 70-79.

Kanuk, Leslie and Conrad Berenson (1975), "Mail Surveys and Response Rates: A Literature Review," *Journal of Marketing Research*, (November), pp. 440-453.

Kaynak, Erdener (1982), *Marketing in the Third World*, New York, N.Y.: Praeger Publishers.

Kelley, Eugene J. and L. Rusty Scheewe (1975), "Buyer Behavior in Stagflation/ Shortages Economy," *Journal of Marketing*, (April), 44-50.

King, William R. and David I. Cleland (1974), "Environmental Information Systems for Strategic Marketing Planning," *Journal of Marketing*, (October), 35-40.

Koch, James V. (1989), "An Economic Profile of the Pacific Rim," *Business Horizons*, March-April, pp. 18-25.

Kotler, Philip (1974), "Marketing During Periods of Shortage," *Journal of Marketing*, (July), 20-29.

____ (1973), "The Major Task of Marketing Management," *Journal of Marketing*, (October), 42-49.

Kunio, Yoshihara (1988). *The Rise of Ersatz Capitalism in South-east Asia*. Oxford University Press: Singapore.

____ (1985). *Philippine Industrialization Foreign and Domestic Capital*. Oxford University Press: Singapore.

Madigan, Kathleen, Gregory L. Miles, Joan O'C. Hamilton and Jonathan B. Levine (1989), "The Expansion: Steady as She Goes," *Business Week*, January 9, pp. 65-67.

Mahal Kong Pilipinas Foundation, Inc. (1989), *Philippines Best 1000 Corporations*, Manila, Philippines: Mahal Kong Pilipinas Foundation.

Martinez, Jon I., John A. Quelch and Joseph Ganitsky (1992). "Don't Forget Latin America," *Sloan Management Review*, Winter, pp. 78-92.

Miller, Matt (1989), "Aquino's Officials Probe Tangled Affairs of Construction Firm Favored by Marcos," *The Asian Wall Street Journal*, (March 20), 20.

____ (1989), "Philippine Request to Paris Clus will Total $1.9 Billion," *The Asian Wall Street Journal*, (March 20), 22.

____ (1989), "Aquino Accepts IMF's Program, Paving Way for $1.3 Billion Loans," *The Asian Wall Street Journal*, (March 13), 3.

____ (1989), "Latest Manila, IMF Negotiations Result in Preliminary Agreement," *The Asian Wall Street Journal*, (February 6), 3.

____ (1989), "Philippines Fails to Privatize its Huge Nickel Mine," *The Asian Wall Street Journal*, (February 6), 3.

____ (1987), "Rescheduling of Manila Debt Appears Likely," *Wall Street Journal*, (October 29).

National Statistical Coordination Board (1989), *Philippine Statistical Yearbook, 1989*, Manila: NSCB.

Paine, George (1992), "Philippines: Infrastructure Equipment is an Export Bright Spot," *Business America*, (April 6), p. 33.

Shama, Avraham (1992), "Managing Marketing during Stagflation in Yugoslavia," *International Marketing Review*, Vol. 9, No. 1, pp. 44-56.

____ (1981), "Coping with Stagflation: Voluntary Simplicity," *Journal of Marketing*, (Summer), 120-134.

___ (1980). *The Impact of Stagflation on Consumer Psychology*. Praeger Publishing: New York.

___ (1978), "Management and Consumers in an Era of Stagflation," *Journal of Marketing*, (July), 43-52.

Shiller, Zachary (1989), "Machine Makers Enjoy the Ride–While it Lasts," *Business Week*, January 9, p. 71.

Shuptrine F. Kelly and Frank A. Osmanski (1975), "Marketing's Changing Role: Expanding or Contracting?" *Journal of Marketing*, (April), 58-66.

Stewart, Thomas A. (1990), "How to Manage in the New Era," *Fortune*, (January 15),58-72.

Thomas, Philip S. (1974), "Environmental Analysis for Corporate Planning," *Business Horizons*, (October) 27-38.

Treece, James B., and Wendy Zellner (1989), "Detroit Tries to Rev Up," *Business Week*, June 12, pp. 78-82.

Trinidad, Arturo Q. (1988), *Zero Equity: Passage to Bankruptcy*, Center for International Affairs, Harvard University, (Boston: New England Publishers Inc.)

Zikmund, William G. (1991), *Exploring Marketing Research*, 4th edition, The Dryden Press.

# APPENDIX A

Survey on the Impact of the
Macroeconomic Environment on Marketing

Name of Company _____

Main Products _____

_____

Name of Respondent _____

Job Title _____

**During the last half of the decade, the Philippine economy has experienced the following economic conditions:**
  **1)** <u>Shortage</u> **of raw materials, supplies, finished goods and foreign exchange,**
  **2)** <u>Slow economic growth,</u> **i.e. growth in GNP,**
  **3)** <u>Inflation,</u> **averaging 15%, in the price of raw materials and finished goods.**
**The inflation rate can also be attributed to the increase in peso prices resulting from a devaluation relative to the U.S. dollar.**

**This questionnaire tries to determine the extent that your firm's marketing strategy is affected as a result of these economic conditions.**

1. How much does a shortage of raw materials and supplies affect your decisions regarding the product line?

    _____ substantially _____ somewhat _____ little _____ none

2. In a situation of raw material shortage, do you offer new products?

    _____ yes (go to #3)
    _____ no  (go to #4)

3. If your answer to #2 is yes, what kind of new products? (Check all that are applicable)

    _____ cheaper, more functional products
    _____ products similar to existing lines
    _____ premium, more expensive products
    _____ other, please specify _____

4. In times of shortage in raw material, do you eliminate products from the line?

    _____ yes (go to #5)
    _____ no  (go to #8)

5. If your answer to #4 is yes, what is the extent of the elimination of products from the line?

    _____ substantially _____ some _____ little

## APPENDIX A (continued)

6.  In times of shortage, which products are eliminated from the line? (Check all that are applicable)

    _____ the highest priced product
    _____ the lowest priced product
    _____ the product with the highest cost to produce
    _____ the product with the lowest cost to produce
    _____ marginal products
    _____ other, please specify product type, _____

7.  Why are products eliminated from the line during times of shortage? (Check all that are applicable)

    _____ shortage of raw materials and supplies
    _____ lower demand for finished output
    _____ competitive action
    _____ other, please specify _____
    _____

8.  When inflation is 15% or more, how much are your selling prices affected? (Place a check mark on the line where applicable)

    a great                      not at
    deal                          all
    |____|____|____|____|____|____|

9.  In response to inflation of 15% or more, how do you adjust your pricing?

    _____ raise peso prices at a rate substantially higher than inflation rate
    _____ raise peso prices at a rate somewhat higher than inflation rate
    _____ raise peso prices at the inflation rate (to keep up with inflation)
    _____ raise peso prices at a rate somewhat below the inflation rate
    _____ raise peso prices at substantially below the inflation rate
    _____ maintain peso prices

10. During inflation of 15% or more, how often do you make changes in your discount policies? (Place a check mark on the line where applicable)

    very                         never
    frequently
    |____|____|____|____|____|____|

11. If changes are made to your discount policies, what type of changes?

    _____ offer new discounts
    _____ increase discounts
    _____ stop discounts
    _____ decrease discounts

12. At what level are pricing decisions finalized?

_____board _____middle _____sales _____sales
    level     managment     manager     force

13. During inflation of 15% or more, how often do you change price differentials among products to change demand? (Place a check mark on the line where applicable)

very                never
frequently
| | | | | |

14. If you do change price differentials to change demand, what is the extent of this change?

_____ all products affected
_____ substantial (more than half of the products are affected)
_____ some (less than half of the products are affected)
_____ minimal

15. When inflation is 15% or more, are changes made in credit decisions?

_____ yes (go to #16)
_____ no  (go to #18)

16. If your answer was yes to #15, by how much will changes be made in consumer credit decisions? (Place a check mark on the line where applicable)

a great         not at
  deal          all
| | | | | |

17. When inflation is 15% or more, what is the extent of this change in consumer credit decisions?

_____ tighten credit extensively
_____ tighten credit somewhat
_____ loosen credit somewhat
_____ loosen credit extensively
_____ no change

18. What do you do about marginal accounts?

_____ drop marginal accounts
_____ cultivate even marginally profitable accounts

19. In response to a shortage of raw materials, do you make changes in your inventory policies?

_____ yes (go to #20)
_____ no  (go to #21)

## APPENDIX A (continued)

20.  If you answered yes in #19, what kind of changes were made?
     _____ accumulate inventory whenever available
     _____ order raw materials only as needed
     _____ other, please specify _____
     _____

21.  Under a condition of shortage, do you reevaluate the suppliers of raw materials?
     _____ yes (go to #22)
     _____ no  (go to #23)

22.  If you answered yes in #21, do you:
     _____ search for new suppliers
     _____ cultivate existing suppliers to get priority treatment
     _____ drop existing suppliers
     _____ other, please specify _____
     _____

23.  How much does a shortage situation affect your research and development (R & D) activities? (Place a check mark on the line where applicable)

     a great                    not at
       deal                       all
     |____|____|____|____|____|

24.  In what way does a shortage situation affect R & D activities?
     _____ substantial increase in R & D activities
     _____ some increase in R & D activities
     _____ no change in R & D activities
     _____ some decrease in R & D activities
     _____ substantial decrease in R & D activities
     _____ stop all R & D activities

25.  What issues are of concern for research and development? (please rank according to (1) highest priority to (4) lowest priority)
     _____ activities are aimed at finding ways to make raw materials go further?
     _____ activities are aimed at using less expensive or lower grade material in production
     _____ activities are aimed at finding substitute materials
     _____ other issues, please specify _____
     _____

The following questions relate to actual implementation of your marketing strategy during a stagflation:

26.  To what extent do you use less expensive (or lower grade) material in production? (Place a check mark on the line where applicable)

     always                     never
     |____|____|____|____|____|

27. To what extent do you invest in research substitute materials? (Place a check mark on the line where applicable)

substantially                    never
|     |     |     |     |     |

28. To what extent do you introduce substitute products? (Place a check mark on the line where applicable)

always                           never
|     |     |     |     |     |

29. As a result of stagflation, are there changes in the composition of your target market?

_____ yes (go to #30)
_____ no  (go to #32)

30. If you answered yes to #29, what was the cause of the change?

_____ the market shifted
_____ our company decided to change our target market
_____ both a market shift and a decision to change the target market
_____ other issues, please specify _____

31. If there are changes in the target market, what was the extent of the these changes? (Check any/all that are applicable)

_____ subtantial change, targeting an entirely different group
_____ adjusting the target group by expanding to other domestic market segments
_____ some change, moderate shifting in the composition of the target group
_____ expansion into the export market

32. How does the current economic situation affect consumer research activities in your firm?

_____ increased consumer research
_____ initiated consumer research activities as a response to the current economic conditions
_____ no change, research activities remain the same
_____ never have performed consumer research activities
_____ decrease in consumer research activities

33. To what extent do you try to find new markets for your goods? (Place a check mark on the line where applicable)

always                           never
|     |     |     |     |     |

34. Do you make any changes in consumer services?

_____ yes, substantial changes were made by adding more services
_____ yes, some services were added
_____ no change in consumer service that are already offered
_____ decrease consumer services
_____ do not offer any consumer service

## APPENDIX A (continued)

35. To what extent do you treat customers selectively in order to maximize loyalty? (Place a check mark on the line where applicable)

selective        similar
treatment       treatment

|___|___|___|___|___|

36. Because of stagflation, to what extent have you been servicing faithful accounts more preferentially than in the past? (Place a check mark on the line where applicable)

preferential      similar
treatment       treatment

|___|___|___|___|___|

37. As compared to other accounts, to what extent have you been servicing faithful accounts better, because of stagflation? (Place a check mark on the line where applicable)

better        same
treatment       treatment

|___|___|___|___|___|

38. To what extent do you increase service to justify a higher price? (Place a check mark on the line where applicable)

substantially      never

|___|___|___|___|___|

Thank you very much for your time and efforts. Please use the enclosed stamped self-addressed envelope for your reply or send the completed questionnaire to:

Juanita Roxas
c/o Antonio V. Roxas
167 Porvenir St.
Pasay, Metro Manila

Completed questionnaires will then be mailed back to the U.S. in batches.

Would you like a copy of the results?

_____ yes
_____ no

Address to send it to: _____
_____

# The Strategies and Characteristics of Exporting SMEs: A Study of Peruvian Firms

### Mercedes Douglas

**SUMMARY.** The behaviour of exporting firms is the result of the complex interaction of many factors of the external and internal environment both at the national and international level. This paper presents the main findings from an exploratory study which assessed the characteristics and marketing strategies of small- to medium-sized exporting firms in a developing country, Peru. Statistical analysis using non-parametric methods to measure the behaviour of these firms used criteria taken from studies of firms in mostly developed countries. The observations from the analysis indicate that characteristics such as size and management perceptions and commitment, and strategies related to market concentration in developed countries taking into consideration export sales volume as a measure of performance (dependant variable) were positively associated to the success of these Peruvian firms and added to their competitiveness. *[Article copies available from The Haworth Document Delivery Service: 1-800-342-9678. E-mail address: getinfo@haworth.com]*

Mercedes Douglas (nee Vásquez Villalobos) is Senior Tutor at the Department of Marketing, University of Strathclyde, Glasgow, UK. She is a member of the Strathclyde International Business Unit and teaches Export and International Marketing. Her main interests are International Marketing and Marketing and Economic Development with particular emphasis in Latin American countries.

[Haworth co-indexing entry note]: "The Strategies and Characteristics of Exporting SMEs: A Study of Peruvian Firms." Douglas, Mercedes. Co-published simultaneously in the *Journal of Global Marketing* (International Business Press, an imprint of The Haworth Press, Inc.) Vol. 9, No. 4, 1996, pp. 35-56; and: *Marketing in the Third World* (ed: Denise M. Johnson, and Erdener Kaynak) International Business Press, an imprint of The Haworth Press, Inc., 1996, pp. 35-56. Single or multiple copies of this article are available from The Haworth Document Delivery Service [1-800-342-9678, 9:00 a.m. - 5:00 p.m. (EST). E-mail address: getinfo@haworth.com].

*35*

## BACKGROUND OF THE RESEARCH

This paper is based on a study conducted in Peru in 1991 which aimed to establish the company and management related factors of export performance of Peruvian firms. The main objective was to complete the profile of macro and micro factors in the Peruvian environment which were important for the performance of exports of non-traditional products. Peru is a country which has relied on exports, particularly of natural resources, since its independence but serious economic and political crisis have curtailed its opportunities for development. The country has seen a continuous deterioration of its exports of traditional products (except in times of boom) and while exports of non-traditional goods are growing an understanding of the factors, beside external economic and socio-political, which affect the behaviour of the firms which manage to survive in such difficult conditions, is necessary. Only with this knowledge can firms assess their strengths and weaknesses to be able to provide for the needs of their customers in a more effective manner.

## REVIEW OF THE LITERATURE

The characteristics of firms and their choice of strategy act as determinants of the performance of firms as well as influencing the initiation and commitment to exporting. The various factors which influence performance have been at the centre of the review of the literature carried out by Aaby and Slater (1988) who devised a model of export performance and their variables.[1] These authors reviewed 55 studies, 30 from the USA and the rest from Canada, Brazil, Norway, Peru, Turkey, West Germany, and the UK. Other countries which the research for this paper looked into were Poland, Jamaica and South Korea. The model highlights in the first instance the dual nature of influences on export performance (the internal and external environments) and the multiplicity of variables which have an impact on it. Any assessment of export performance should take all these into consideration. In this study the following constituents of firms' characteristics were examined: size (number of employees, total sales); management commitment measured in terms of attitudes and perceptions of the influence of external factors and of export operations; and experience (years in business as well as exporting). The researcher also investigated issues concerning strategies such as selection of market numbers and adaptation of the marketing mix.

The criteria used to measure performance also varies in all these studies and it is mostly elusive. Many use the exporter versus the non-exporter criteria without considering financial objectives such as growth and profitability. Others consider the export sales volume criteria in order to define size and compare the different groups according to the impact that size has on performance. Other studies consider non-financial aspects such as motivation as predictor or determinant of success.

## *Characteristics*

Commitment to exports, experience and attitudes have been found by the majority of studies considered for this research to be the underlying reasons for the successful development of exporting–including high and positive expectations and motivation–[Cavusgil (1984), Young et al. (1989), Thomas & Araujo (1985), Amine & Cavusgil (1986), Bradley (1990), Madsen (1989), Axinn (1988), Bilkey (1982), Aaby & Slater (1989), Majaro (1991), Weaver & Pak (1990), Cooper & Kleinschmidt (1985)]. The perception of exporting as a potentially advantageous activity influences the motivation of the management and the allocation of resources.

Only a limited number of studies have found a significant association between size and export performance [Christensen et al. (1987) and Tookey (1964)] although it is believed that larger firms are better equipped to survive and have better financial and credit opportunities. As far as perceptions towards support for exports studies carried out in developing countries argue that this is crucial for success [Fonfara & Collins (1990), Weaver & Pak (1990), Christensen et al. (1987), Nicholls et al. (1988) and Kaynak and Erol (1991)]. The general perception is that the experience of firms in developing economies is more complex because they are at an earlier stage of internationalisation and may be introducing products which are already in the mature stage of PLC$^2$ in western markets, therefore their need for support is obviously higher. Daniels and Robles (1982) in their study of the Peruvian textile industry viewed the role of the government as a conditioning factor which forced companies to define their choice of technology and the market destination for their products. With regard to support from official organisations, Bodur and Cavusgil (1985) and Weaver and Pak (1990) found out that they were not widely used because they did not provide exporters with information specific to their needs. Government incentives in developed countries are viewed as impediments to export in studies by Rao et al. (1990), Sriram et al. (1989), and Sullivan and Bauerschmidt (1988).

Diamantopoulos (1988), Christensen et al. (1987) and Crick (1992) argue that such a diverse range of findings and attitudes to support, either by government or other agencies could be the result of the different companies researched, their different stage in their export involvement (internationalisation) as well as the market being served. The evidence regarding the role of government and other organisations' support points to its importance for firms which are at the initial stages of internationalisation but later on its role must change and become more specific to different needs that arise at different stages and in different circumstances.

## Strategies

The literature on this area is concerned with the policies the firm has for selection of markets overseas as well as the determination of marketing strategies and tactical issues of the marketing mix. The importance of appropriate strategies has been emphasised by Darling (1988), Segler (1987) and Nicholls et al. (1988) and many other authors for example, Kotler (1988), and Albaum et al. (1989) and Piercy (1982) who advocate for more attention to these elements in order to perform better in international markets. This study is concerned with the choice of market numbers and the adaptation of the marketing mix.

## Market Selection

The research in this area has concentrated mainly on western companies and has centred on the debate about the need to either concentrate or spread/diversify. Choosing the right numbers of markets allows the company to understand possible competitive developments. It has also implications for allocation of resources [Albaum et al. (1989)] which is seen as a determinant of success [Papadopoulos (1988) and Tookey (1964)] and is correlated to growth [Piercy (1982) and Cooper & Kleinschmidt (1985)]. Furthermore high involvement, committed exporters tend to go to more markets and more different locations than low-involvement exporters [Diamantopoulos (1988)]. Lee and Yang (1990) however, found no significant difference between selection of numbers and sales growth and profitability. They observed however, that those firms following a strategy of diversification/spreading or concentric diversification had a better export performance that those who concentrated on few markets.

## Marketing Mix Adaptation

The main objective of investigations regarding product, promotion, distribution and pricing policies has been the adaptation versus standardisation theme. Although Baker and El-Dessuki (1982) found that adaptation of the marketing mix elements is very significantly associated to higher export performance in terms of export sales ratio and profitability, not all mix elements have been studied or found to be associated to performance.

Cooper and Kleinschmidt (1985) and Rice and Reid (1985) maintain that world marketers' growth and higher performance can be associated to product adaptation or a high degree of product diversification to suit the needs of the markets. On the other hand Christensen et al. (1987), although agreeing that product quality was a key element of success, this was also related to product standardisation. Amine and Cavusgil (1986) argued that performance improves with less product adaptation and Cavusgil and Kaynak (1982) also observed that product was the least adapted element in his survey of manufacturing firms in Canada.

As far as adaptation of promotion is concerned, there is a limited amount of empirical research carried out in this area. Cavusgil and Kaynak (1982) in his study of success factors observed that promotion required more adaptation and it was important for success and Madsen (1989) found a relationship between communication and sales, growth and profitability. The preoccupation of writers and researchers in this area concentrates on the effects of the different promotional tools used in the export markets, their degree of standardisation/adaptation and also the general impact of communication on export performance [Czinkota & Johnston (1983), Buckley et al. (1990), Rice & Reid (1985), Amine & Cavusgil (1986) and Kirpalani & Robinson (1989)].

The importance of distribution and entry mode is widely recognised because the success or failure of exporting depends on securing orders from buyers and delivering them on time, in the best condition and receiving payments. It has been found that the practice is very much inclined towards adaptation although its impact on success offers yet again conflicting conclusions [Albaum et al. (1989), Amine & Cavusgil (1986)]. The use of intermediaries is very common amongst SME (Paliwoda, 1986) and is an important factor in export policy. Madsen (1989) as well as Bilkey (1982), Cavusgil and Kaynak (1982), and Kirpalani and Robinson (1989) observed that channel support was associated to sales and growth and was an important factor of success.

The pricing element is regarded as either a profitability, competitive or marketing tool [Amine & Cavusgil (1986), Cooper & Kleinschmidt (1985), Madsen (1989)] As with the other factors of the marketing mix, findings vary widely. Rao et al. (1990) and Rice and Reid (1985) argued that competitiveness depended on price adaptation/adjustment. Christensen et al. (1987) observed that successful exporters relied on international competitive prices and used internal factors to make pricing decisions. Others like Buckley et al. (1990) observed that price competition could be forced on firms and cost performance had to be achieved through product rationalisation. Cavusgil and Kaynak (1982) found a weak association between pricing and success.

## RESEARCH METHODOLOGY

The study was basically exploratory combined with descriptive and analytical research using both secondary and primary research. By the nature of the investigation qualitative and quantitative data was sought. Both have advantages and disadvantages associated with depth of understanding and meaning, objectivity, degree of standardisation and measurability.

The population frame was obtained from four sources: the Directory of Exportable Offer (1988/89) published by the Institute for Foreign Trade (ICE), the Directory of Exporters published by the Association of Peruvian Exporters and two lists published by the ICE one regional and one national. The firms represented a cross section of exporters from the different areas regarded as non-traditional.[3] The most active industries in the non-traditional sectors in 1988 were agriculture (farming and livestock, flowers), textiles, chemicals, sider-metallurgy, wood and paper.

A mail questionnaire was sent to 105 firms. Ninety-three questionnaires were posted but only 64 were confirmed to have been received. Thirty-four questionnaires were returned which translates into a response rate of 53%. Twenty-five responses (39%) came from active exporters of non-traditional products: agriculture (9), fishing (4), textiles (4), metal machinery (2), chemical (1), non-ferrous minerals (2), leather products (1), handicrafts (2). These were analysed using SPSSx to carry out two types of non-parametric tests: Spearman and Mann-Whitney U.

The investigation was limited by sparse information regarding exporting activities at the micro level in less developed countries as has been already explained. There is, however, a wide range of investigations carried out for developed countries and most of the criteria used in this area was applied to this present research. It was hoped that the field research would also allow the researcher to ascertain whether the behaviour of the exporter in a developing country can be measured using the same tools as those used in developed countries and to explain the reasons behind their performance.

This study like many exploratory ones did not intend to be a predictive study but rather descriptive making use of empirical inputs. The performance of firms is still highly linked to external factors like the economic and political situation. This environment is particularly difficult in Peru which continues to perform poorly within the international context. The particular attributes of these exporting firms however should allow them to continue producing similar results to those observed in the study.

The study limited itself to a small number of exporters taken from all industries involved in non-traditional exports. Like any cross sectional approach it lacks depth and cannot be generalised by industry. The performance of the firms studied was measured mainly in terms of sales volume (total and exports) for three years which may pose limitations for long term observations and growth analysis. This means that the findings are based on performance averages which lack precision. The companies were mostly small or medium sized and for reasons or confidentiality more precise information about their performance was difficult to obtain.

The study concentrated on experienced firms so the findings will have to be taken with certain degree of reservation as there were no studies in Peru regarding new exporters, non-exporters or unsuccessful exporters at the time of the research. It also applies to companies in the fishing and agricultural sectors to a large extent since the majority of responses came from this sector. The study offers a limited historical perspective and cannot provide insights into the sustainability of future performance.

## FINDINGS

### 1. Characteristics

Firm characteristics included factors related to certain attributes which are specific to the firm and others to the management. Firm specific attributes refer to the size of the firms determined in terms of sales volume and number of employees. Management characteristics were defined by their commitment (status of the decision maker, experience and attitudes towards exporting) and exporting motivation, initial and present, for exports. Part of their examination of attitudes was concerned with their perceptions to support for exports. This refers to specific policies such as tax incentives and the support by other organisations, through the services designed to help export activities.

The perceived importance of success factors refers to the perceptual evaluation of the various elements of business performance. It is based on the assumption that any action towards achieving success is directly or indirectly related to how important these elements are perceived to be.

This section establishes in the first instance the firms' profile, growth rates and commitment through their motivation and attitudes to exports and in the second, if these factors–including size and perceptions of the impact of support and incentives–are statistically associated to performance. The profile of the respondents was made according to industry, size, type of firm and age. The responses came mainly from the agricultural and fishing sectors (13 firms) which as it happens were the area which showed a higher growth rate than any other sector (3.4% in 1988). Ninety-four percent of firms used mixed technology and 90% were independent of which 6 were at the experimental stage, 5 at the intermediate and 14 were experienced exporters. Nine firms had achieved growth of up to 50%, 4 more than 100% and even those which experimented no change (4) could be said to have been successful to survive in a country with very difficult economic and political conditions.

The mean (average earnings) for the first year was $6.6 million and for the second £7.1 million. This indicates an average growth of 9.2%. The measure of performance used was export and total sales over three years. This was used in order to establish the size of the exporters. The problem was that the sample was too small and it was analysed in an aggregate form. The findings then consider only the performance of the larger firms, and in this sense it is biased. Questions on profitability, by reasons of confidentiality were not raised in the questionnaire in financial but in perceptual terms: respondents were asked about the expected rate of growth and whether profits had met their expectations for the years under consideration.

In order to establish the financial and non-financial benefits regarding their involvement in exporting the perceptions of participants about its effect on a number of specific factors were also investigated. The purpose of this was to differentiate between financial and non-financial benefits accrued from exporting. It can be assumed that financial gains are at the core of any business operation and, in effect profitability was cited by 15 firms as being the most important motive for continuing exporting. However, many firms will continue to export even if their profits had not met their expectations, for other important reasons which could be part of the company's goals (Albaum et al., 1989). Likert-type scaled questions were asked to indicate whether exporting had had a very negative (1) or very positive (5) impact on other areas. Between 16 and 18 firms considered that the areas which had positive and very positive benefits from exporting were market presence, stability and commitment and to a lesser extent profits (13 out of 25 firms).

*Size*

This was defined by number of employees and size of total sales volume and both measures indicated that the majority of firms were in the small to medium size category which had between 26 to 250 employees and sales volume between $1 million to $25 million. Twenty-two firms (84%) belong to the SME category–a further breakdown indicates that 36% had sales volumes of below $1 million and 48% of up to $25 million. Fourteen companies had between 26 and 250 employees. It had not been possible to select the sizes of the firms before the survey but as it happened, the responses came from firms predominantly in the SME group. This could either mean that the non-traditional sector is dominated by SMEs or that large companies did not want to take part in the survey. The size of the non response could not be established.

It was interesting to observe that size of the company in terms of number of employees is positively correlated to export performance (Table 1) which suggests that Peruvian firms which were larger within this group of SMEs had higher export sales volumes than the smaller ones ratifying the findings of other researchers [Christensen et al. (1987) and Tookey (1964)]. Firms between 101 and 850 (which include 9 large firms with more than 250) employees accounted for exports valued at over $148 million for 1989 and over $160 million in 1990. In terms of growth ratios, however, it was SMEs between 15 and 249 employees which grew at a rate of over 15% compared to 8% by large firms. No direction of causality could be established so it is possible that better performance levels could be incidental, however, it is likely that these firms enjoy advantages associated with greater capacity of production, access to finance and managerial resources. Size cannot be considered in isolation since better performance could also be attributed to their experience in exporting and commitment. These firms are also responsible for the sales of agricultural and fishing products an area which the Peruvian government would like to continue developing.[4]

*Commitment*

This is related to the desire to start or continue exploiting export activities and it depends on experience as well as of managerial attitudes and motivations. The majority of firms in the study (14) were experienced exporters, sold more that 50% of their output overseas the decisions were taken at high management levels. Their increased exposure to international markets had evidently benefited them as the statistical analysis indicates (see Table 2). Experience allows firms to acquire better knowledge of the markets and their own capabilities but also to be able to prove if their

TABLE 1. Correlations with Size

| Performance Measures | Number of Companies | Value of Correlation* |
|---|---|---|
| Export Sales: 1989-1990 | 25 | 000 |
| 1990-1991 | 25 | 000 |
| 1991-1992 | 25 | 025 |

*significance at 5%

positive expectations about exporting and profitability can be matched by reality.

In the table below the significant positive correlation emphasises the association which exists between these firms' experience and their performance corroborating the findings of Bradley (1990), Madsen (1989), Axinn (1988), Amine and Cavusgil (1986) and Bilkey (1982).

*Motivation* has been found to be correlated to performance by several researchers because it is related to commitment [Young et al. (1989), Thomas and Araujo (1985) and Amine and Cavusgil (1986)]. The dimensions instrumental to motivation are managerial characteristics—since motivation tends to originate from decision makers—and actual reasons for initiating and staying in exporting. The motivation of Peruvian firms were examined in order to determine how reactive or proactive, or systematic, the firms tended to be when assessing existing markets or screening potential ones. Differentiation between these motives is relevant for defining the behaviour of firms, to see how important these factors are for export activities (Albaum, 1989), what other goals firms pursue through exports, and if they can be related to performance (Cooper and Kleinschmidt, 1985).

Respondents were given a list of variables to establish their initial and current motives for exporting. Table 3 indicates the frequencies and mean ranks obtained which shows that with the exception of managerial pressure all others were perceived to be important motivational factors.

The most striking finding, however, was the negative association between declining domestic sales and saturated domestic market (both reactive motives) and both total and export sales volume for the three years under consideration (see Table 4). The results imply that the performance of reactive firms have been less successful; however, even though the impact of proactive motives has not been statistically proven it could be affirmed that in an indirect manner proactive reasons have better effects on firms' results.

If the perceptual view of the respondents is taken as a measurement of success then these firms are highly committed to exporting because they

### TABLE 2. Correlations with Years in Exporting

| Factor | Performance Measures | | Value of Correlation* |
|--------|---------------------|---|----------------------|
| Years in Exporting | Export Sales: | 1989-1990 | 000 |
| | | 1990-1991 | 000 |
| | | 1991-1992 | 009 |

*significance at 5%

TABLE 3. Initial and Current Motives—Frequencies and Means

| Motives | Valid Cases | Initial Motives: Mean Scores | Valid Cases | Current Motives: Mean Scores |
|---|---|---|---|---|
| Competitive pressures (p) | 7 | 4.2 | 8 | 3.6 |
| Exclusive market infomration (p) | 8 | 3.5 | 10 | 4.1 |
| Overcapacity (r) | 9 | 3.2 | 9 | 3.7 |
| Managerial pressure (p) | 7 | 2.0 | 7 | 2.8 |
| Declining domestic sales (r) | 10 | 3.6 | 12 | 3.1 |
| Saturated domestic market (r) | 9 | 3.3 | 10 | 3.0 |
| Profitability (p) | 19 | 4.0 | 15 | 3.9 |
| Marketing advantages (p) | 16 | 4.0 | 16 | 4.3 |
| Proximity to ports (r) | 8 | 3.0 | 8 | 3.0 |
| Design/technology advantages (p) | 10 | 4.0 | 14 | 4.0 |
| Overseas enquiries (r) | 16 | 4.1 | 17 | 4.0 |

Note: (p) proactive, (r) reactive

TABLE 4. Correlations with Declining Domestic Sales and Saturated Domestic Market

| Factors | Performance Measures | | Number of Companies | Value of Correlation* |
|---|---|---|---|---|
| Declining Domestic Sales | Export Sales: | 1989-1991 | 12 | − .005 |
| | | 1990-1991 | 12 | − .024 |
| Saturated Domestic | Export Sales: | 1989-1990 | 10 | − .029 |
| | | 1990-1991 | 10 | − .013 |

*significance at 5%

have remained in it for a long time, their expectations are high and their motivations, proactive.

*Government Incentives and Services Offered by Other Organisations.* Findings of the study in this area were also striking. The perceptions of the respondents, who believe that the assistance of the government is vital for their success (mean of 3.4), and the statistical tests were contradictory because the use of grants for example–although its use was limited to a small number of firms–was negatively associated to performance suggesting the less successful performance of those firms which used them (Table 5). The impact of tax incentives (albeit a very weak negative significance at 10%) puts into question the effectiveness of such measure for this group of firms. Ten out 22 responses view the use of tax incentives as important and very important for their performance, and 8 of them were experienced exporters. For 12 respondents its importance was limited. This suggests that it is highly likely that this type of incentive is inappropriate to the needs and experience of firms [Bodur & Cavusgil (1985), Weaver & Pak (1990), Crick (1992)].

Organisations such as the Peruvian Exporters Association (ADEX), banks, the Institute of Foreign Trade (ICE), distributors and agents abroad were perceived to be valuable for exporters. ICE, which has been dismantled was more highly rated by companies based in the north of Peru. It is possible that the relevant office in this area was more accessible to firms which could not get information and did not have contacts in the capital where the majority of exporters have their own offices. The statistical analysis however, only finds positive associations with ADEX. Associations between performance and the impact of Banks is of very low significance (Table 6).

With the exception of banks where interest had increased, their intended future use was lower which could ratify the findings that as firms become more experienced they rely less on these organisations.

Respondents were also given a list of 18 services and from these only export training was found to be associated to better sales performance emphasising its already recognised importance by those involved in exporting. As with government incentives the aggregate use of the services was found to have significant negative associations to sales (Table 7).

### TABLE 5. Correlations with Government Incentives

| Factors | Performance Measures | Number of Firms | Significance |
|---|---|---|---|
| tax incentives | Export Sales 1989-1991 | 20 | − .055 |
| grants | Growth<br>Growth | 5 | − .008*<br>− .016* |

*significance at 5%

### TABLE 6. Correlations with Other Organisations Used by the Firms

| Factors | Performance Measures | | Number of Companies | Value of Correlation[a] |
|---|---|---|---|---|
| ADEX | Export Sales | 1991-1992 | 17 | .031[b] |
| Banks | Export Sales | 1989-1990 | 18 | .053 |

a:  Mann-Whitney U Test, 2 tailed, corrected for ties
b:  signifiance at 5%

This is of high relevance insofar as the impact of support for exports because the results of this study support the extant research findings in most studies in developed countries which argue for a more discriminate set of measures for exporters according to their size and experience. Market information and finance are still a problem for these exporters in Peru.

The findings in this section will add to the controversy surrounding the effects of the support given to exporters by the government and other organisations. The government, an external element in the performance model, is perceived to have a facilitating role which can create positive perceptions (internal factor) but whose intervention cannot be associated to the success of the firms in our study.

## 2. Strategies

Findings on market numbers and the adaptation of marketing mix are examined in this section.

### Number of Export Markets

With regard to the selection of numbers of markets it appears that a concentration strategy was used by the majority of respondents since 18 of them exported to less than 12 countries.[5] The correlations established by the test show a significant association with performance (Table 8). This however could simply mean that these markets are allowing the company to maintain their level of sales but whether more markets would improve their performance in other areas is not established. It could be argued that because these companies have been in operation for a long time, they have had the opportunity to choose and concentrate on their best markets which explains their better performance. On the other hand the study does not indicate that the number of markets reached have been purposely selected therefore no definite conclusion can be made. What is important concerning markets is the direction of trade.

TABLE 7. Aggregate Use of Organisations—Correlations

| Performance Measure | | Value of Correlation* |
|---|---|---|
| Export Sales: | 1989-1990 | − .030 |
| | 1990-1991 | − .002 |

*significance at 5%

TABLE 8. Number of Countries—Correlations

| Performance Measures | Spearman Correlations* |
|---|---|
| Export Sales:  1989-1990 | .005, .002 |
| 1990-1991 | .021, .001 |

*significance at 5%

Although between 12 and 15 companies sell in South America and North America, a higher proportion of their sales go to the EEC (9 firms out of 13 sold more than 40% to European countries in 1991). Most of the Western European countries and two of the three North American ones are linguistically and culturally different to Peru. The only significant association at 5% with performance was found to be with North America (at .007 and .003) which is not surprising since Peru has a long established and successful trade relationship with the USA.

*Adaptation of the Marketing Mix*

Companies were asked if they had carried out any changes to their marketing mix in order to export and what effect these had had on specific exporting activities. The majority of respondents did not effect any changes, 8 adapted product and 7 adapted price and communication, only 4 adapted distribution.[6] It was also observed that 6 respondents had adapted both product and price although the reasons for this were not altogether clear.

Respondents were also asked to indicate whether adaptation of the marketing mix improved or worsened their profit and other non-financial factors. The list of factors and mean ranks are given in Table 9.

With the exception of profits, distributions and sales methods, communications, technology transfer and risk spreading all other factors had very high mean scores (3.5 or above) which reflects the perception of the respondents that changes to the mix had a considerable effect on these areas. The specific effects of adaptation on these factors were not discussed but in another section of the study pricing was seen as an important performance factor although it was affected by the high production costs in the country. The need for improvements on product and production methods can be understood because these factors are of great consequence for export competitiveness in international markets specially if those markets are in the developed countries which require more sophisticated products. Although profits had not improved, their general performance in export markets in terms of export presence, knowledge of their customers

TABLE 9. Effects of Marketing Mix Adaptation on Profit and Non-Profit Factors

| Factors | Mean Ranks |
| --- | --- |
| distribution and sales methods | 3.1 |
| risk spreading | 3.2 |
| profits | 3.3 |
| technology transfer | 3.3 |
| communications | 3.4 |
| price | 3.5 |
| product and production methods | 3.6 |
| number of export markets | 3.6 |
| market presence | 3.6 |
| stability for the firm | 3.7 |
| knowledge of customers | 3.7 |
| long term opportunities | 3.8 |
| sales in export markets | 3.8 |
| commitment to exports | 3.9 |

Note: Likert-type scale (1: much worse, 3: neither worse nor better, 5: much better)

and sales were found to be better as well as their stability, the opportunities for the longer term and the companies' commitment to continue in exporting. It can therefore be argued that these firms' attitude to exporting had been positively influenced by adaptation, even though the statistical associations with general performance were weak.

These findings on marketing factors are not as conclusive as the ones observed in many of the studies discussed in our literature review. If we consider these firms in the light of Rao's findings (1990) they can be defined as affected intensifiers because they are likely to be highly influenced by the recessionary situation of the country. In this case they would only carry product modifications because of tactical rather than strategic reasons. However there is no evidence that pricing is used to manipulate sales which is a characteristic of affected intensifiers. Therefore it can be assumed that the majority of these firms which are exporters only and do not rely in the internal, Peruvian market use product modification as part of their strategy for exports.

## IMPLICATIONS

This study has highlighted the associations which exist between the performance of Peruvian firms and some of their characteristics and strategies. The commitment of these Peruvian exporters has been enhanced by the positive perceptions of the management regarding exports, their perceived proactive motivations and their experience notwithstanding that the statistical correlates were not significant at the levels required for this study. The implications for managers and policy makers is that it is necessary to maintain this positive attitude and reinforce it by means of adequate back up and opportunities to continue in exports. These internal, management related qualities have not been diminished by the critical situation of the country thus it could be expected that if conditions improved better results may occur and even if they were to remain the same this performance could be replicated by other companies.

On the question of size the evidence of a beneficial association with larger size in terms of number of employees implies that these firms have possibly accrued advantages such as a larger staff to cope with international operations. The fact that the majority are small or medium-sized indicate their particular skills for survival and a better knowledge of their problems and capabilities. This is of particular importance for the country because these firms are mostly financed from national sources and they are responsible for the fastest growing exporting sector: the sales of agricultural and fishing products. Because they are responsible for products coming from different areas of the country they are also contributing to promote decentralisation. Problems such as weakness in planning, access to funds, training and technology acquisition for those which are not in the agribusiness sector need to be adequately addressed and understood. More research is required in firms of the same size in the individual industrial sectors and also to ascertain the direction of causality between size and performance.

The most striking implication is drawn from the attitudes and associations to export support. The managers have a very defined idea about the importance of the support they have and want from the government but the use of incentives such as tax and grants did not benefit the firms who had better performance. Given the size and experience of the firms this implies that the advantages accrued from export support, whether governmental or not, are relative. This depends on the different needs that originate from the time they have been in business and their resources hence they require specific support and services. This ratifies the literature review carried out in most developed countries and in Brazil.

As far as choice of market numbers and adaptation of the marketing mix is concerned the performance of the firms in the study does not offer any clear conclusions. Their exports sales performance was not associated to strategic issues such as adaptation of the marketing mix but although adaptation was not correlated to success the perceptions of the respondents concerning its importance were high. It is likely that the changes to products were made before the products were taken to the market and had not been sold previously in their unchanged version for the customers to have been able to establish a comparison or to have any direct relationship to sales.

On the question of market numbers, it was not possible to clarify whether the tendency to concentrate on a few number of markets, which was positively correlated to performance was a deliberate strategic choice, however because their markets are mainly in developed countries, it could be argued that they have managed to choose their best markets where they have established a productive presence.

## CONCLUSIONS AND RECOMMENDATIONS FOR FURTHER RESEARCH

This paper has provided empirical results from a study of Peruvian SME exporting firms. It contributes to fill a gap in the Peruvian export literature by investigating the export behaviour and the factors associated with export success. It also adds to the knowledge concerning experienced small-to-medium sized firms in developing countries, an area which has received very limited attention in terms of research. The study corroborates previous research concerning the characteristics, choice of markets and adaptation/standardisation strategies of successful firms. The performance of the Peruvian firms investigated is linked to their internal characteristics and their concentration on markets in developed countries. Furthermore the research expands on previous studies by examining various background factors and recognising the multifactor nature of behaviour and performance. It concludes that those internal, firm/management-related factors should serve as the basis for policy making and decisions for export support. This will give opportunities for a more effective and efficient use of scarce resources by differentiating firms and their needs.

The key research propositions tested were related to two groups. The first dealt with firms' and managements' characteristics and posited positive associations between size, experience, commitment, export support and perceptions towards exporting. Size and experience in terms of years in business and exporting were quantifiable variables. Other such as commitment, attitudes and motives were mostly perceptual and open to bias.

The performance of small-to-medium sized firms was observed in the research and the relationship between better performance and larger firms within the group was established. It is necessary to study a larger sample of the same group to give a more universal validity to a similar cross-sectional study. On the other hand industry specific studies are also needed

52

and because of the economic and geographical division of the Peruvian economy studies looking at the different regions is also advisable.

The findings also show that experience in terms of the years in exports and the experience of managers interact to influence export performance. Further research should be carried out to find out more about the profiles of firms which have just started exporting and also of those firms which are not yet exporting but which may have export potential.

On the issue of motivation, the associations were negative and concerned reactive motives. These findings need to be explored further using a larger sample in order to establish a profile of those firms motivated in this manner and their performance.

Related to the above and also to size is the question of the impact that support for exports may have on exporters. In our study the use of tax incentives and grants were negatively associated to performance. CERTEX had been used by firms whose volume of exports decreased between 1989-91 or did not export at all. In the case of one firm the tax was never reimbursed; in another the firm run into liquidity problems once the tax incentive ceased to exist. All the firms which had used CERTEX and were not successful (9) cited financial problems caused by internal costs as well as unstable exchange rates as their most critical problems. Other issues, for example to what use this incentive was put to was not looked into. According to López (1987) firms which tend to use this very transparent incentive tend to export in order to get the incentive rather than as a genuine interest in export development. More research is necessary to investigate the reasons for this in terms of the nature of the support, the organisations involved since the Institute of Foreign Trade (ICE) ceased to operate, the impact this has had on exporters, and the support needs of the firms according to their various experience and size levels in a larger sample.

The study also concentrated on resource-based industries which have been recognised in the export promotion efforts of the government as a significant source of growth but it is also needed to look at the manufacturing sector which is the basis of the industrial development of the country.

The question of ownership needs also to be looked differently since the findings of this study considered only firms which are locally owned and financed. The influence of ownership by international organisations is also important not only from the view of financial sourcing but also on the aspects related to transfer of technology and business practices.

The second group of propositions concerned marketing strategy and propounded positive associations between performance and selection of market numbers and choice of adaptation or standardisation. Significant correlations were found with choice of concentration in developed countries. The most successful market was found to be North America. It is therefore necessary to carry out further research into those areas were no associations were found and to study the performance of firms and the reasons for this in the most popular markets as well as in others. This is important if exporters view choice of markets and numbers as an important strategic tool and the result of careful screening.

Marketing issues such as adaptation which did not produce conclusive evidence needs to be studied in more detail. This study did not consider other factors such as the marketing orientation of the firms nor or the impact this may have on performance.

Although a limited number of characteristics is discussed in this paper, it offers a contribution to export marketing and management literature by providing empirical data from Peru, demonstrating the importance of those background characteristics and the fact that firms from a developing country can be investigated using the same tools as those used in developed countries.

These variables were studied from the exporters point of view, that is the supply side which is only one side in the network of suppliers and buyers. The performance of exporters needs also to be measured from the demand side for a more complete equation and to have a more complete assessment of Peruvian exporters. For this it would be necessary to contact the customers of these firms in a sample of countries in order to establish how they are perceived and what their performance is in their international markets. This can be done at the level of intermediary or final customer and will require setting up further studies.

On a more general focus, one of the most important conclusions in this study is that although conditions in Peru are very difficult, exporters from developing countries are able to behave and perform in a similar manner to those in more developed countries where firms enjoy a more stable environment. The experience of other firms in similar countries could be expected to follow similar patterns.

On the basis of the study, it can therefore be concluded that size, commitment, experience and concentration on developed countries are of considerable importance for export performance.

Further research is necessary in a number of areas. As stated previously a larger sample with more participants from the various industries could be used to replicate this cross-sectional study in Peru and other developing economies. Alternative methodologies using longitudinal research is also necessary to investigate the evolution and behaviour of the firms over time and the factors that trigger change and to give more depth to this type of research.

## NOTES

1. This is not a model for research in itself but a summary of the factors which have been seen to influence performance.

2. PLC: Product life cycle.

3. This is the way the Peruvian government has classified non-traditional products and includes agriculture, textiles, fishing, machinery and metal products, chemical, metallurgy, non metallic minerals, wood and paper, leather, handicrafts.

4. SMEs are considered to be important to economic development because they are likely to employ a larger sector of the population than in developed countries and can act as a means to restore the balance between agriculture and industry because they can create an infrastructure of invention and innovation. They can also promote decentralisation and encourage domestic market expansion.

5. The definition of concentration used was that of Lee & Yang (1990).

6. High and very high adaptation (4 and 5 in the Likert-type scale).

## REFERENCES

Aaby, N. and Slater, S., (1989) "Management Influences on Export Performance: a Review of the Empirical Literature 1978-88," *International Marketing Review*, 6, 4, 7-26.

Albaum, G., Strandskov, J., Duerr, E., and Dowd, L., (1989) *International Marketing and Export Management*, UK: Addison Wesley Publishers Ltd.

Amine, L., and Cavusgil, T., (1986) "Export Marketing Strategies in the British clothing Industry." *European Journal of Marketing*, 20, 7, 21-23.

Axinn, C., (1988) "Export Performance: Do Managerial Perceptions Make a Difference?," *International Marketing Review*, 5, 2, 61-71.

Baker, M. J. and El Dessuki, A-Z., (1982) *Successful Exporting*, Westburn Publishers Ltd.

Bilkey, W., (1982) "Variables Associated with Export Profitability," *Journal of International Business Studies*, Fall, 39-55.

Bodur, M., and Cavusgil, T., (1985) "Export Market Research Orientations of Turkish Firms." *European Journal of Marketing*, 19, 2, 8-16.

Bradley, F., (1991) *International Marketing Strategy*, UK: Prentice Hall International Ltd.

Buckley, P. J., Pass, C. L., Prescott, K., (1990) "Measures of International Competitiveness: Empirical Findings from British Manufacturing Companies," *Journal of Marketing Management*, 6/1, 1-14.

Cavusgil, T., (1984) "Organizational Characteristics Associated with Export Activity," *Journal of Management Studies*, 21, 1, 3-22.

Cavusgil, T. and Kaynak E., (1982) "Success Factors in Export Marketing: an Empirical Analysis, An Assessment of Quality Thought and Practice," *Educators' Conference Proceedings*, American Marketing Association, Chicago, 48, 309-312.

Christensen, C., da Rocha, A. and Gertner, R., (1987) "An Empirical Investigation of the Factors influencing Exporting Success of Brazilian Firms." *Journal of International Business Studies*, Fall, 61-77.

Cooper, R. and Kleinschmidt, E., (1985) "The Impact of Export Strategy on Export Sales Performance," *Journal of International Business Studies*, Spring, 37-55.

Craig, R. and Beamish, P., (1989) "A Comparison of the Characteristics of Canadian and UK Exporters by Firm Size," *Journal of Global Marketing*, 2, 4, 49-6.

Crick, Dave, (1992) "UK Export Assistance: are we supporting the best programmes?," *Journal of Marketing Management*, 8, 81-92.

Czinkota, M. and Johnston, W., (1983) "Exporting: does Sales Volume make a Difference?," *Journal of International Business Studies*, Spring/Summer, 147-153.

Daniels, J. and Robles, F., (1982) "The Choice of Technology and Export Commitment: The Peruvian Textile Industry," *Journal of International Business Studies*, Spring/Summer, 67-87.

Darling, J., (1985) "Keys for success in Exporting to the US Market," *European Journal of Marketing*, 19, 2, 17-27.

Dichtl, E., Koeglmayr, H. and Mueller, S., (1990) "International Orientation as a Precondition for Success," *Journal of International Business Studies*, 21, 1, 23-40.

Diamantopoulos, A., (1988) "Identifying Differences between High- and Low-Involvement Exporters," *International Marketing Review*, Summer 52-60.

Fonfara, K. and Collins, M., (1990) "The Internationalisation of Business in Poland," *International Marketing Review*, 7, 4, 86-99.

Jatusripitak, S., (1984) *The Exporting Behavior of Manufacturing Firms*, UK: UMI Research Press, Library of Congress.

Kaynak, E. & Erol, C., (1991) The Export Propensity of Turkish Manufacturing and Trading House Firms, *Journal of Marketing Management*, 5, 211-229.

Keegan, Warren. (1984) *Multinational Marketing Management*, 3rd edn, Prentice Hall.

Kirpalani, V. and Robinson W., (1989) "The China Market and Lessons from Successful Exporters," *Journal of Global Marketing*, 2, 4, 81-98.

Lee, C. and Yang, Y., (1990) "Impact of Export Market Expansion Strategy on Export Performance," *International Marketing Review*, 7, 4, 41-51.

López de la Piniella, J., (1987) *El Trueque en el Siglo XXI*, Edición IPGH, Mexico.

Madsen, T., (1989) "Successful Export Marketing Management: Some Empirical Evidence," *International Marketing Review*, 6, 4, 41-57.

Majaro, S., (1991) "International Marketing–The Main Issues" in Baker, M., *The Marketing Book*. Oxford: Butterworth-Heinemann.

Nicholls, J., Lyn-Cook, M. and Roslow, S., (1988) "Strategies for Export Marketing of Non-traditional Products" *International Marketing Review*, 6, 4, 58-72.

Paliwoda, S., (1986) *International Marketing*, London: Heinemann.

Piercy, N., (1982) *Export Strategy: Markets and Competition*, Allen and Unwin.

Rao, C., Erramilli, K. and Ganesh, G., (1990) "Impact of Domestic Recession on Export Marketing Behaviour," *International Marketing Review*, 7, 2, 54-65.

Rice, G. and Reid, G, (1985) Canadian Export Marketing in North Africa, *EMAC Proceedings*, Bielefeld, 129-139.

Segler, K., (1987) "The Challenge of Basic Strategies," *European Journal of Marketing*, 21, 5, 76-89.

Sriram, V., Neelankavil, J. and Moore, R., (1989) "Export Policy and Strategy Implications for Small-to-Medium Sized Firms," *Journal of Global Marketing*, 3, 2, 43-60.

Sullivan, D. and Bauerschmidt, A., (1988) "Common factors Underlying Incentive to Export: Studies in the European Forest Products Industry," *European Journal of Marketing*, 22, 10, 41-55.

Thomas, M. and Araujo, L., (1985) "Theories of Export Behaviour: A Critical Analysis," *European Journal of Marketing*, 19, 2, 42-52.

Tookey, D., (1964) "Factors associated with Success in Exporting," *The Journal of Management Studies*, March, 48-66.

Weaver, M. and Pak, J., (1990) "Export Behaviour and Attitudes of Small- and Medium-sized Korean manufacturing Firms," *International Small Business Journal*, 8, 4, 59-70.

Young, S., Hamill, J., Wheeler, C. and Davies, R., (1989) *International Market Entry and Development, Strategies and Management.* England: Harvester Wheatsheaf.

# Marketing Adaptations by American Multinational Corporations in South America

Surjit S. Chhabra

**SUMMARY.** The extent of international marketing mix adaptations by American MNCs has been an unresolved issue despite numerous commentaries and articles. A major contributor to this state has been the paucity of empirical research on this issue. An investigation was undertaken to assess the extent of adaptations in twenty-three marketing mix elements in fifty-eight MNCs operating in South America. The results show that the MNCs adapt their pricing and promotion elements the most and their product and distribution elements the least. Also, the MNCs make obligatory adaptations in the developing countries of South America rather than discretionary adaptations. *[Article copies available from The Haworth Document Delivery Service: 1-800-342-9678. E-mail address: getinfo@haworth.com]*

## INTRODUCTION

American Multinational Corporations (hereafter referred to as MNCs) operating in foreign markets have long been faced with the task of trans-

Surjit S. Chhabra holds a DBA in marketing from Indiana University. His research interests are in international marketing standardization/globalization and health care marketing. His articles have appeared in the *Journal of Ambulatory Care Marketing*. Formerly an assistant professor in marketing at DePaul University where he taught courses in Marketing Management, International Marketing and Global Economy, he is now an independent consultant.

[Haworth co-indexing entry note]: "Marketing Adaptations by American Multinational Corporations in South America." Chhabra, Surjit S. Co-published simultaneously in the *Journal of Global Marketing* (International Business Press, an imprint of The Haworth Press, Inc.) Vol. 9, No. 4, 1996, pp. 57-74; and: *Marketing in the Third World* (ed: Denise M. Johnson, and Erdener Kaynak) International Business Press, an imprint of The Haworth Press, Inc., 1996, pp. 57-74. Single or multiple copies of this article are available from The Haworth Document Delivery Service [1-800-342-9678, 9:00 a.m. - 5:00 p.m. (EST). E-mail address: getinfo@haworth.com].

*57*

ferring their marketing program to their foreign markets. Their choices range from having an identical marketing program to a completely different or adapted marketing program, or a strategy somewhere in-between these two extremes wherein some elements of their marketing program are adapted to the local tastes/environment and some others are extended without any adaptation (Buzzell 1968; Jain 1989; Keegan 1969; Killough 1978; Quelch & Hoff 1986; Walters 1986). Despite a longstanding debate presenting arguments for adaptation (Donnelly, Jr. 1970; Fournis 1962; Marcus 1964; Lenormand 1964; Ryans, Jr. 1969), and against adaptation (Elinder 1964; Dunn 1976; Fatt 1964; Miracle 1968; Roostal 1963; Levitt 1983), the issue remains far from being resolved in part due to a lack of empirical evidence about the extent of marketing mix adaptations by the MNCs. Only a handful of empirical studies have been undertaken in the last three decades (Aydin & Terpstra 1981; Aylmer 1968; Boddewyn, Seohl & Picard 1986; Hansen & Boddewyn 1976; Hill & Still 1984; Kackar 1974; Siddiqi 1976; Sorenson & Wiechman 1975; Terpstra 1967; Wind, Douglas, & Perlmutter 1973). Another shortcoming of the past literature is that most of the empirical studies have concentrated only on the developed countries of Western Europe. Developing countries, with their unique features such as the existence of dual economy, wide inequality between the rich and the poor in terms of income and wealth, limited infrastructural development and often times extraordinary circumstances (for example, the hyperinflation in Brazil) present several additional factors that impinge on the decision to adapt the marketing mix variables over and above the normal product-market and company-subsidiary related factors. Only five studies (Aydin & Terpstra 1981; Grosse & Zinn 1990: Hill 1980; Kackar 1974; Ozsomer, Bodur & Cavusgil 1991) have examined the marketing program transfers by the American MNCs to the developing countries. Last but not least, the empirical research has virtually ignored pricing and distribution adaptations.

This study was undertaken to fill these voids. The extent of adaptations in twenty-three marketing mix elements listed in Table 1 (representing product, promotion, distribution, and pricing elements) in South America was studied with fifty-eight American MNCs.

## RESEARCH HYPOTHESES

Three hypotheses culled from the literature on international marketing standardization were tested in this study. This section discusses these hypotheses and the rationale behind them.

## TABLE 1. Marketing Mix Elements Used in the Study

**Product Elements:**
Product Size
Product Features
Product Ingredients/Materials
Number of Models in the Product Line
Product Label
Product Brand Name/Symbol
Product Packaging

**Promotion Elements:**
Promotional Theme
Creative Expression (commercials, print advertisements, brochures, etc.)*
Use of Media Mix (T.V., radio, magazines, etc.)
Media Allocations (proportionate dollars spent on media)
Use of Special Promotions (coupons, rebates, trade shows, etc.)
Structure of the Sales Force (product specialists, territory specialists, etc.)
Commission/Incentives Paid to the Sales Force
Role Played by the Sales Force (order taking, problem
solving, shelf-stocking, etc.)

**Distribution Elements:**
Type of Middlemen Used (distributors, agents, retailers, etc.)
Functions Performed by the Middlemen (taking title, financing, advertising, etc.)
Levels of Distribution (direct-to-customer, agent-to-retailer, etc.)
Distribution Objectives (minimize costs, on-time-delivery, etc.)

**Pricing Elements:**
Trade Margins
Expected Return on Investment
Price Level
Pricing Strategy (meet-the-competition, above-the-competition, etc.)

*The examples provided in the parentheses were also included in the questionnaire

1. Varying degrees of adaptation are expected for the different elements of the marketing mix. Specifically, pricing and promotion elements are hypothesized to be adapted the most, followed by distribution and product elements (Akaah 1991; Grosse & Zinn 1990; Quelch & Hoff 1986; Walters 1986). Product elements, namely, brand name, product ingredients, and product features are expected to be least adapted due to the significant costs associated with such adaptations. Research evidence examining the adaptation of product mixes by MNCs across countries indicates this to be the case (Aydin & Terpstra 1981; Boddewyn et al. 1986; Hill & Still 1984; Kackar 1974; Onkvisit & Shaw 1989; Rosen 1989; Sorenson & Wiechman 1975).

2. Greater adaptation is expected for consumer products than for industrial products. This hypothesis has been discussed and supported
   the most in the debate on international marketing standardization
   (Bakkar 1977; Boddewyn et al. 1986; Hansen & Boddewyn 1976;
   Jain 1989; Keegan 1969; Miracle 1968; Rau & Preble 1987; Sorenson & Wiechman 1975; Walters 1986). The rationale for this hypothesis is that industrial goods are generally more amenable to
   economies of scale and the universality of their buying motives lend
   them to greater standardization. Consumer products' sales, however,
   depend more upon local consumers' tastes and preferences and
   hence would have to be more adapted. A contrary perspective is offered by Levitt (1983) in which he argues that consumers' tastes and
   preferences worldwide are converging to high quality (brand name)
   goods at the lowest possible prices due to the advances in communication technology and increased cross-border travel. However, the
   evidence of such convergence is anything but overwhelming (Boddewyn et al. 1986).
3. Greater marketing mix adaptation is expected in larger markets
   (Brazil in our study) than in smaller markets (Venezuela in our
   study). Grosse and Zinn (1990, p. 62) provide the logic behind this
   hypothesis, ". . . cost reductions that are achieved through standardization are expected to be more important in smaller markets, where
   sales are less likely to cover the added costs of adaptation than in
   larger markets."

## *METHODOLOGY*

Three hundred eighty-six MNCs with subsidiaries and/or affiliates in
South America were selected from the Directory of American Firms with
Operations Overseas. Only MNCs that sold tangible products were included. The Chief Foreign Officer (or equivalent) in these MNCs were
contacted via telephone to request their cooperation in filling out the
questionnaire. The MNCs on the list were then mailed a packet containing
a questionnaire, return envelope, feedback request form, and a description
of the terms used in the questionnaire. Approximately six weeks later a
follow-up wave of mailings was conducted. Sixty-eight MNCs returned
the questionnaire. However, nine of the returned questionnaires were un-
usable due to substantial non-completion and one arrived too late to be
included in the study. The final sample of 58 MNCs represented a broad
spectrum in terms of sales and types of products. A comparison of respondents with non-respondents revealed no significant differences in types of

product, size, and the extent of their globalization. It should also be mentioned that the sample size of 58 MNCs is more than twice the size of the next largest sample of MNCs (27 MNCs in consumer packaged goods industry) employed in a study of international marketing standardization in United States-based MNCs (Sorenson & Wiechman 1975).

The questionnaire used in the study included the twenty-three marketing mix elements detailed in Table 1 and asked the respondents to choose a product that their MNC first sold in the United States and now also sells in South America and indicate whether each of the 23 elements was the same or different in their "lead" country (their most important market in South America) compared with the home (United States) market. Sixty-eight percent of the respondents chose the principal product of their MNC (defined as the product that accounted for the largest percentage of the MNC's worldwide sales). The respondents were also asked to check the reasons for adaptations, if any, in each of the 23 elements. The reasons for adaptation included obligatory reasons (governmental regulations, market infrastructure, product use conditions and language) and discretionary reasons (customers' preferences, customers' income levels, and attitude toward American products/MNCs). The questionnaire also collected data on regional marketing standardization and marketing decision making centralization. The questionnaire was extensively pretested with the Chief Foreign Officers of seven MNCs in personal interviews lasting an average of one and a half hour each. The data collection, including the pretest, was done in mid-to-late 1988. The situation in the two countries involved in this study–Brazil and Venezuela–may be somewhat different now. Admittedly, this is a limitation–albeit a minor one–of this study.

## HYPOTHESES TESTING AND RESULTS

Hypotheses 1 and 2 were tested by examining the extent of marketing mix adaptations by American MNCs in South America categorized by type of product. Tables 2-4 report the extent of marketing mix adaptations by the respondent MNCs and the top two leading reasons for adaptations in each element. Hypothesis 3 was tested by examining the extent of marketing mix adaptations by American MNCs in Brazil (57% chose Brazil as their lead country) and in Venezuela (24% chose Venezuela as their lead country). These are reported in Tables 5 and 6. The other countries chosen as the lead countries were: Argentina (7%), Chile (3%), and Colombia (7%).

TABLE 2. Product Adaptations by American MNCs in South America

| Product Element | Total | % Adapting (n) Cons. | Ind. | Leading Reasons for Adaptation |
|---|---|---|---|---|
| Models in line | 66% (53) | 72% (18) | 63% (35) | 1. Product use conditions<br>2. Customer preferences |
| Packaging | 49% (55) | 63% (16) | 44%[a] (39) | 1. Language<br>2. Product use conditions |
| Size | 38% (55) | 56% (18) | 30%[b] (37) | 1. Customer preferences<br>2. Product use condition |
| Label | 30% (54) | 35% (17) | 27% (37) | 1. Language<br>2. Govt. Regulations |
| Features | 19% (57) | 28% (18) | 15% (39) | 1. Product use condition<br>2. Customer preferences |
| Ingredients | 15% (55) | 18% (17) | 13% (38) | 1. Govt. Regulations<br>2. Product use conditions |
| Brand name | 7% (57) | 11% (17) | 5% (40) | 1. Customer preferences<br>2. Language |

[a]$p = < .10$ [b]$p = < .05$

Legend:
% Adapting = Percentage of respondent MNCs adapting the marketing mix element in each cell
(n) = Total number of respondent MNCs in each cell
Cons. = Consumer products
Ind. = Industrial products

### Product Adaptations

It appears from Table 2 that American MNCs adapt the models in their product line the most in South America, followed by product packaging and product size. This is not surprising since in most developing markets, discretionary incomes are limited, necessitating adaptations in product line, size and packaging to enable the customers to afford the "luxury" products offered by the MNCs. For instance, Warner-Lambert, which sells Chiclets chewing gum in 12-piece packs in the United States, decided to sell 2-piece packs for the equivalent of a few cents each in Latin America (Hill & Still 1984, p. 95). On the other hand, products oriented to families must appear in larger sizes in developing markets due to the existence of extended families and higher fertility rates.

The least adapted product element was the brand name. It appears that

TABLE 3. Promotion Adaptations by American MNCs in South America

| Promotion Element | Total | % Adapting (n) Cons. | Ind. | Leading Reasons for Adaptation |
|---|---|---|---|---|
| Use of sales promotion | 80% (49) | 89% (18) | 74%[a] (31) | 1. Market infrastructure<br>2. Customer preferences |
| Media allocation | 76% (50) | 83% (18) | 72% (32) | 1. Market infrastructure<br>2. Product use condition |
| Use of media mix | 72% (47) | 78% (18) | 69% (29) | 1. Market infrastructure<br>2. Language |
| Creative expression | 72% (53) | 72% (18) | 71% (35) | 1. Language<br>2. Customer preferences |
| Incentives to sales force | 72% (53) | 78% (18) | 69% (35) | 1. Market infrastructure<br>2. Customers' incomes |
| Structure of sales force | 60% (53) | 67% (18) | 57% (35) | 1. Market infrastructure<br>2. Product use conditions |
| Promotional theme | 52% (54) | 67% (16) | 44%[a] (38) | 1. Customer preferences<br>2. Market infrastructure |
| Role played by sales force | 44% (54) | 59% (17) | 38%[a] (37) | 1. Market infrastructure<br>2. Customer preferences |

[a]$p = < .10$

Legend:
%  Adapting = Percentage of respondent MNCs adapting the marketing mix element in each cell
(n) = Total number of respondent MNCs in each cell
Cons. = Consumer products
Ind. = Industrial products

Levitts' (1983) assertion about the globalization of markets is becoming true in at least the marketing subset of branding as other researchers have also found evidence of increasing global branding practices on the part of MNCs (Boddewyn, Seohl & Picard 1986; Hill & Still 1984; Onkvisit & Shaw 1989; Rosen, Boddewyn & Louis 1989; Sandler & Shani 1992; Sorenson & Wichman 1975). A recent study of Fortune 500 companies shows that more than 20% of these companies develop brand names because of their ability to cross international borders (Sandler & Shani 1992,

TABLE 4. Distribution and Pricing Adaptations by American MNCs in South America

| Marketing Element | Total | % Adapting (n) Cons. | Ind. | Leading Reasons for Adaptation |
|---|---|---|---|---|
| **Distribution:** | | | | |
| Functions performed | 50% (48) | 38% (16) | 56% (32) | 1. Market infrastructure 2. Customer preferences |
| Levels of distribution | 43% (53) | 50% (18) | 40% (35) | 1. Market infrastructure 2. Product use condition |
| Type of middlemen | 41% (46) | 41% (17) | 41% (29) | 1. Market infrastructure 2. Product use condition |
| Distribution objectives | 28% (50) | 31% (13) | 27% (37) | 1. Market infrastructure 2. Product use conditions |
| **Pricing:** | | | | |
| Price level | 82% (55) | 89% (18) | 78% (37) | 1. Market infrastructure 2. Govt. Regulations |
| Trade Margins | 81% (53) | 83% (18) | 80% (35) | 1. Market infrastructure 2. Govt. Regulations |
| Expected return on investment | 79% (54) | 78% (18) | 81% (36) | 1. Market infrastructure 2. Govt. Regulations |
| Pricing Strategy | 46% (54) | 39% (18) | 49% (36) | 1. Government Regulations 2. Market infrastructure |

Legend:
  % Adapting = Percentage of respondent MNCs adapting the marketing mix element in each cell
  (n) = Total number of respondent MNCs in each cell
  Cons. = Consumer products
  Ind. = Industrial products

p. 29). The universal appeal and success of Levi's, McDonald's and Coke undoubtedly is an inspiration for such a practice. This lends support to hypothesis 1. Hypothesis 2 was also supported for product elements since the levels of adaptation for product elements were lower for industrial products than for consumer products (Boddewyn, Seohl & Picard 1986; Jain 1989; Samiee & Roth 1992; Sorenson & Wiechman 1975).

American MNCs appear to be making obligatory adaptations in their product elements in South America to a much larger extent than discre-

TABLE 5. Marketing Mix Adaptations by American MNCs in Brazil versus Venezuela

| Marketing Mix Element | % Adapting: (n) Brazil | % Adapting: (n) Venezuela | Sig. |
|---|---|---|---|
| **Product:** | | | |
| Product size | 42% (33) | 25% (12) | ns |
| Product features | 24% (33) | 14% (14) | ns |
| Product ingredients | 22% (32) | 8% (12) | ns |
| Models in product line | 77% (31) | 50% (12) | p = < .10 |
| Product label | 26% (31) | 21% (14) | ns |
| Brand name | 9% (33) | 7% (14) | ns |
| Product packaging | 53% (32) | 36% (14) | ns |
| **Promotion:** | | | |
| Promotional theme | 61% (31) | 31% (13) | p = < .10 |
| Creative expression | 84% (31) | 54% (13) | p = < .05 |
| Use of media mix | 77% (30) | 50% (10) | p = .10 |
| Media allocation | 84% (31) | 45% (11) | p = < .01 |
| Use of special promotions | 71% (31) | 100% (10) | p = .05 |
| Sales force structure | 56% (32) | 83% (12) | p = < .10 |
| Sales force incentives | 74% (31) | 85% (13) | ns |
| Sales force role | 42% (31) | 64% (14) | ns |
| **Distribution:** | | | |
| Type of middlemen used | 34% (29) | 50% (12) | ns |
| Role of middlemen | 38% (29) | 75% (12) | p = < .05 |
| Levels of distribution | 42% (31) | 54% (13) | ns |
| Distribution objectives | 21% (28) | 42% (12) | ns |
| **Pricing:** | | | |
| Trade margins | 84% (31) | 64% (14) | ns |
| Expected return on investment | 81% (32) | 69% (13) | ns |
| Price levels | 90% (31) | 71% (14) | p = .10 |
| Pricing strategy | 47% (32) | 50% (14) | ns |

Legend:
    Sig. = Significance; ns = not significant

TABLE 6. Marketing Mix Adaptations by Amercian MNCs in Brazil versus Venezuela by Type of Product

| Marketing Mix Element | % Adapting: (n) Consumer Products | | | | % Adapting: (n) Industrial Products | | | |
|---|---|---|---|---|---|---|---|---|
| | Brazil | | Venezuela | | Brazil | | Venezuela | |
| Product size | 60% | (10) | 40% | (5) | 35% | (23) | 14% | (7) |
| Product features | 30% | (10) | 20% | (5) | 22% | (22) | 11% | (9) |
| Product ingredients | 22% | (9) | 20% | (5) | 22% | (23) | 0% | (11) |
| Models in product line | 80% | (10) | 80% | (5) | 70% | (23) | 29% | (7)[b] |
| Product label | 33% | (9) | 20% | (5) | 23% | (22) | 22% | (9) |
| Brand name | 10% | (10) | 20% | (5) | 8% | (23) | 0% | (9) |
| Product packaging | 67% | (9) | 60% | (5) | 48% | (23) | 22% | (9) |
| Promotional theme | 80% | (10) | 40% | (5) | 52% | (21) | 25% | (8) |
| Creative expression | 80% | (10) | 60% | (5) | 86% | (21) | 50% | (8)[b] |
| Use of media mix | 80% | (10) | 60% | (5) | 75% | (20) | 40% | (5) |
| Media allocation | 90% | (10) | 60% | (5) | 81% | (21) | 33% | (6)[c] |
| Use of special promotions | 80% | (10) | 100% | (5) | 67% | (21) | 100% | (5) |
| Sales force structure | 60% | (10) | 100% | (5)[a] | 55% | (22) | 71% | (7) |
| Sales force incentives | 80% | (10) | 100% | (5) | 71% | (21) | 75% | (8) |
| Sales force role | 67% | (9) | 60% | (5) | 32% | (22) | 67% | (9)[a] |
| Type of middlemen used | 33% | (9) | 60% | (5) | 35% | (20) | 43% | (7) |
| Role of middlemen | 33% | (9) | 50% | (4) | 40% | (20) | 88% | (8)[c] |
| Levels of distribution | 60% | (10) | 40% | (5) | 33% | (21) | 63% | (8) |
| Distribution objectives | 25% | (8) | 60% | (5) | 19% | (21) | 29% | (7) |
| Trade margins | 90% | (10) | 60% | (5) | 81% | (21) | 75% | (8) |
| Expected return on investment | 80% | (10) | 60% | (5) | 82% | (22) | 75% | (8) |
| Price level | 90% | (10) | 80% | (5) | 90% | (21) | 67% | (9) |
| Pricing strategy | 50% | (10) | 40% | (5) | 45% | (22) | 56% | (7) |

[a]p = < .10;   [b]p = < .05   [c]p = < .01

tionary adaptations, as the obligatory reasons for adaptation (language, governmental regulations, and product use conditions) were cited more often than the discretionary reasons (customer preferences).

### Promotion Adaptations

Table 3 reports the results of promotional mix adaptations by the American MNCs in South America. Use of special promotions is adapted the most with 80% of the respondents reporting adaptation in their use of special promotions in this region. This is understandable since a lot of the governments in South America restrict the use of certain kinds of sales promotions (Boddewyn 1988), and sales promotion is generally not as sophisticated overseas as it is in the United States (Ball & McCulloch 1990). Sociocultural and economic constraints also necessitate adaptations in American MNCs' use of sales promotions in the South American markets. For instance, premiums are often stolen from the products and sold separately for extra income in the Latin markets. A gadget to be used in the kitchen will be valued by the American housewife but will not be particularly attractive to a Latin American housewife if she has two maids to do the housework (Ball & McCulloch 1990. p. 485). In many Latin American nations, however, contests, raffles and games have been extremely successful because people love to play the odds.

Media allocation and use of media mix also show high levels of adaptation. This is hardly surprising since a marketing manager is unlikely to encounter the plethora of media choices in the Latin American market that he/she has in the United States market. Television, the key medium in the United States market, is often limited as an advertising medium in the South American markets. Sociocultural factors would also dictate adaptation in media mix and allocation. For example, in Venezuela, the existence of a strong middle class and an elite class, coupled with one of the highest literacy rates in Latin America (the highest literacy rate in Latin America is in Costa Rica), would necessitate increased use of print media. Brazil, too, offers a plethora of print media–over 900 newspapers alone (Ball & McCulloch 1990). Table 3, however, indicates that most American MNCs make adaptations in their media mix and allocation due to market infrastructural differences as it was cited as the leading reason for adaptations made in these two marketing mix elements.

Our study also lends support to the pattern standardization hypothesis of Peebles, Ryans, and Vernon (1978). Fifty-two percent of the respondents reported adapting the promotional theme. However, the creative expression (television ads, print ads, etc.) adaptation was reported by 72% of the MNCs. It appears that a substantial number of American MNCs transfer their basic promotional themes from the home (United States) market to the South American markets and let their subsidiaries tinker with the creative execution as long as the basic promotional theme is held constant. This was especially applicable in the industrial goods category where only 44% of the respondents reported adapting their promotional theme.

Considerably lower levels of adaptation were reported for structure of sales force and the role played by the sales force. Generally, American MNCs make less adaptations in these elements as they establish their operations overseas. For instance, when the Amway corporation, which specializes in direct sales, opened its sales subsidiary in Argentina, it used the same structure and role played by its sales force in Argentina as it does in the United States market. Earlier, it had also transferred its direct sales apparatus to the Mexican and Brazilian markets with minimal adaptations (Maas 1993).

The higher levels of adaptation in the promotional mix elements by the American MNCs in their South American markets lend support to hypothesis 1. Consistently higher levels of adaptation in promotional mix elements for consumer products also confirm hypothesis 2.

### Distribution and Pricing Adaptations

Distribution elements, along with product elements, are hypothesized to be the least adapted elements of a marketing mix when an MNC ventures overseas (Jain 1989; Sorenson & Wiechman 1975; Walters 1986). Our study confirms this hypothesis. The four distributional elements reported adaptation percentages ranging from 28% for distribution objectives to 50% for functions performed by the middlemen (Table 4).

Functions performed by the middlemen (taking title, financing, advertising, etc.) were adapted the most. This may be due to the fact that the middlemen in the Latin American nations are not as sophisticated as in the United States market. Also, in some countries of South America, for example in Venezuela, there are some very strong cartels in the distribution (wholesaling) sector that thwart any standardization attempts by the MNCs (Wade 1993).

Less than half the respondents reported making adaptations in levels of distribution and the type of middlemen being used. One of the reasons for lower levels of adaptations in these two elements maybe that MNCs often bypass the local distribution system in the developing countries in favor of transferring their distribution system from the home market. The fifth largest Dutch firm, SHV Holdings, has successfully opened hypermarkets in Venezuela and Brazil even though the concept of hypermarkets was alien to these markets until its introduction by SHV Holdings (Wade 1993). Even lower levels of adaptations in these two elements of distribution should be expected in the future in the Latin American markets because of a proliferation of American style franchising. For instance, in Brazil, American style franchising is a $30 billion business having grown 30% in each of the last two years. Recent entrants into the field include Kentucky Fried Chicken, Domino's Pizza and the Arby's chain (Tristan 1993).

Interestingly, MNCs reported the lowest level of adaptations (28%) for distribution objectives. It appears that American MNCs do not compromise on their distribution objectives (e.g., on-time delivery, customer service, etc.). This may be an impetus to bypass the local distribution system and transfer the home country's distribution system to the South American markets as was the case with Amway and SHV Holdings.

Pricing elements are usually the most adapted elements in transferring a marketing mix abroad (Jain 1987; 1989; Ball & McCulloch 1990). Predictably, price level, trade margins and expected return on investment were three of the most adapted marketing mix elements reported by the American MNCs. Adaptations in these elements are often necessary due to the differences in labor costs, distribution costs, and interference by the local governments. In Brazil, for instance, the government has instituted price controls on numerous occasions in an attempt to control hyperinflation (Kamm 1993). American MNCs, however, attempt to implement the same pricing strategy (meet-the-competition, prestige pricing, etc.) as in the home market. Much lower levels of adaptations were reported in Table 4 for pricing strategy. One contributing factor to this may be the emergence of global competition from the same competitors that forces the MNCs to adopt a consistent pricing strategy across markets.

Overall, the data in Tables 2-4 constitute support for hypotheses 1 and 2.

### Brazil versus Venezuela

Tables 5 and 6 report the extent of marketing mix adaptations by the American MNCs in Brazil and Venezuela-the top two "lead" countries for American MNCs in the South American region-and test hypothesis 3.

In Table 5, all of the product elements and most of the promotional and pricing elements are adapted to a higher extent in Brazil, and a number of these differences in proportions are statistically significant. The same pattern holds when adaptation levels are compared by type of product between these two countries (Table 6). The product and promotional elements may have to be adapted more in Brazil due to high inequality of income distribution, low per capita income, and lesser developed infrastructure (Haggerty 1993; Nyrop 1983). Venezuela has higher per capita income, literacy rate, standard of living, and lower social class mobility barriers as compared with Brazil (Haggerty 1993). In this regard, Venezuela is closer to the United States market hence facilitating more standardization of marketing mix transfers by the American MNCs.

Also, as Grosse and Zinn (1990) pointed out, the size of the Brazilian market may play a crucial role in American MNCs adapting most of their marketing mix elements to a greater extent in Brazil than in Venezuela. American MNCs may deem Brazil to be a sufficiently large market for their products to recoup the costs of product and promotion adaptations and to maximize their sales in what is the largest market in South America. Venezuela, with a population of only about 20 million, despite a per capita income of US\$ 3,100 in 1993 (higher than that of Brazil), is still too small a market for American MNCs to undertake higher cost adaptations in product and promotion elements.

However, it is interesting to note that for marketing mix elements requiring lower cost of adaptation (e.g., use of special promotions, sales force structure, sales force incentives, sales force role, and all four elements of the distribution mix), American MNCs exhibit greater levels of adaptation in Venezuela than in Brazil. This suggests that American MNCs are guided primarily by cost considerations in adapting their marketing mix elements (assuming that the other factors remain constant, for instance, the "psychic-distance" between the host market and the home market) to their foreign markets. And, the size of the market becomes a proxy for such cost considerations.

With fourteen of the twenty-three marketing mix variables exhibiting greater levels of adaptation for Brazil, the data in Tables 5 and 6 lend at least partial support to hypothesis 3.

## DISCUSSION AND IMPLICATIONS

This study fills an important void in the literature on international marketing mix adaptations by the United States-based MNCs. It studies the adaptations made by the United States-based MNCs in all four of their marketing mix variables (product, promotion, distribution, and pricing) in the developing countries of South America, whereas most of the empirical studies in the past have focused on product and promotion adaptations in Western Europe only (Aylmer 1968; Boddewyn, Soehl, & Picard 1986; Britt 1974; Hansen & Boddewyn 1976; Sorenson & Wiechman 1975; Terpstra 1967; Wiechman 1976).

The study confirms the finding in the literature that the United States-based MNCs adapt their product elements the least (Boddewyn, Soehl, &

Picard 1986; Sorenson & Wiechman 1975) and their pricing elements the most (Hansen & Boddewyn 1976) in their foreign markets. More recently, Grosse and Zinn (1990) and Akaah (1991) also found similar results in their studies of international marketing strategy transfers. The product elements found to be least adapted (brand name, product ingredients, and product features) in this study are the same that Sorenson and Wiechman (1975, p. 40) found to be most standardized in their study of 27 consumer packaged goods MNCs. The MNCs included in this study represented consumer durables, consumer non-durables, industrial parts/materials, industrial capital goods, and industrial supplies, indicating that the aforementioned product elements are adapted the least across a wide spectrum of products. This is hardly surprising since trademark/logo protection and uniform brand image are usually highly coveted by the MNCs (Sorenson & Wiechman 1975, p. 40-41).

Another oft-reported finding in the literature, that consumer products are adapted to a higher extent than industrial products, is also confirmed by our study. For nineteen of the twenty-three marketing mix elements studied, consumer goods marketers reported higher levels of adaptation.

It also appears from our data that the American MNCs engage in obligatory adaptations more so than discretionary adaptations because the obligatory reasons of market infrastructure, governmental regulations, language and product use conditions were cited as the leading reasons for adaptations much more often than the discretionary reasons of customers' preferences, customers' income levels and attitude toward American products/MNCs.

As the Latin American markets develop their infrastructures, and the governments begin to liberalize their economies, less adaptations of marketing mixes should be expected by the American MNCs in these markets. In addition, the Latin consumer market is a young market (about 56% of the population is under 24 years of age), an aspirational market (Latin consumers are attracted to novelty and to the comforts and status symbols they see among their counterparts in the developed world), and is fast becoming a pan-regional market (Business Latin America 1993). Future research should focus on uncovering the extent of region-wide marketing mix standardization by the American MNCs in this region and the variables associated with such a strategy.

## REFERENCES

Akaah, I.P. (1991). Strategy Standardization in International Marketing: An Empirical Investigation of its Degree of Use & Correlates. *Journal of Global Marketing*, Vol. 4(2), 39-62.

Aydin N. and Terpstra V. (1981). Marketing Know-how transfers by MNCs: A Case Study in Turkey, *Journal of International Business Studies*, 12 (Winter), 35-48.

Aylmer, R. J. (1968). Marketing Decision Making in the Multinational Firm. *Unpublished Doctoral Thesis*, Harvard Business School.

Bakkar, B.A. (1977). International Marketing Standardization. *Presentation to European International Business Administration Annual Meeting*, December, 1-21.

Ball, D.A. & McCulloch Jr., W. H. (1990). *International Business: Introduction and Essentials*. Business Publications Incorporated, Homewood, Illinois.

Boddewyn, J.J. 1988. *Premiums, Gifts, Competitions and Other Sales Promotions*. New York: International Advertising Association.

Boddewyn, J.J., Soehl, R., and Picard J. (1986). Standardization in International Marketing: Is Ted Levitt in Fact Right? *Business Horizons*, 29 (November-December), 69-75.

Britt, S.H. (1974). Standardizing Marketing for the International Market, *Columbia Journal of World Business*, 9 (winter), 39-45.

Business Latin America. (1993). *The New Latin Consumer*. April 19.

Buzzell, R.D. (1968). Can You Standardize Multinational Marketing, *Harvard Business Review*, 46 (November-December), 102-113.

Donnelly, J.H. (1970). Attitudes Toward Culture and Approach to International Advertising, *Journal of Marketing*, 34 (July), 60-63.

Dunn, S.W. (1976). Effect of National Identity on Multinational Promotional Strategy in Europe, *Journal of Marketing*, 40 (October), 50-57.

Elinder, E. (1964). How International Can Advertising Be? In S. Watson Dunn (Ed.) *International Handbook of Advertising* (pp. 12-16). New York: McGraw Hill Book Co.

Fatt, A.C. (1964). The Danger of 'Local' International Advertising, *Journal of Marketing*, (January).

Fournis, Y. (1962). The Markets of Europe or The European Market? *Business Horizons*, 5 (Winter), 77-83.

Grosse, R. & Zinn, W. (1990). Standardization in International Marketing: The Latin American Case. *Journal of Global Marketing*, Vol. 4(1), 53-78.

Haggerty, R.A. (ed.). 1993. *Venezuela: A Country Study*. Federal Research Division. Library of Congress.

Hansen, D.M. and Boddewyn, J.J. (1976). American Marketing in the European Common Market, 1963-1973, *European Journal of Marketing*, vol. 11, #7.

Hill, J.S. (1980). Product and Promotion Adaptions in Lesser-Developed Countries. *Unpublished Doctoral Dissertation*. University of Georgia, Athens.

Hill, J.S. and Still R. (1984). Adapting Products to LDC Tastes, *Harvard Business Review*, (March-April), 92-101.

Jain, S.C. (1987). *International Marketing Management*. Kent Publishing Company. Boston, Massachusetts.

Jain, S.C. (1989). Standardization of International Marketing Strategy: Some Research Hypotheses. *Journal of Marketing*, Vol. 53 (January), 70-79.

Kackar, M.(1974). *Marketing Adaptations of U.S. Business Firms in India*. New Delhi: Sterling Publishers Pvt. Ltd.

Kamm, T. (1993). Brazil's Reluctant President Reaches End of First Tumultuous Year in Office. *The Wall Street Journal*. Friday, October 1.

Keegan, W.J. (1969). Multinational Product Planning: Strategic Alternatives, *Columbia Journal of World Business*, 33 (January), 58-62.

Killough, J. (1978). Improved Payoffs From Transnational Advertising, *Harvard Business Review*, 56 (July-August), 102-110.

Lenormand, J.M. (1964). Is Europe Ripe for the Integration of Advertising? *International Advertiser*, Vol. 5 (March).

Levitt, T. (1983). The Globalization of Markets, *Harvard Business Review*, (May-June), 92-102.

Marcus, C. (1964). France. In S. Watson Dunn (Ed.) *International Handbook of Advertising*, New York: McGraw Hill Book Co.

Maas, P. (1993). Argentina: Amway Moves In. *Business Latin America*. April 19.

Miracle, G.E. (1968). Internationalizing Advertising: Principles and Strategies, *MSU Business Topics*, 16 (Autumn), 29-36.

Nyrop, R.F. (ed.). (1983). *Brazil: A Country Study*. Foreign Area Studies. The American University.

Onkvisit, S. & Shaw, J.J. (1989). The International Dimension of Branding: Strategic Considerations and Decisions. *International Marketing Review*. Vol. 6. No. 3.

Ozsomer, A., Bodur, M. & Cavusgil, S.T. (1991). Marketing Standardization by Multinationals in an Emerging Market. *European Journal of Marketing*. Vol. 25, No. 12.

Peebles, D.M., Ryans, Jr., J.K. & Vernon, I.R. (1978). A New Perspective on Advertising Standardization. *European Journal of Marketing*. Vol. 11. No. 8.

Quelch, J.A. and Hoff E.J. (1986). Customizing Global Marketing, *Harvard Business Review*, 64 (May-June), 59-68.

Rau, P.A. & Preble, J.F. (1987). Standardization of Marketing Strategy by Multinationals. *International Marketing Review*, Autumn, 18-28.

Roostal, I. (1963). Standardization of Advertising for Western Europe, *Journal of Marketing*, 27 (October), 15-20.

Rosen, B.N., Boddewyn, J.J. & Louis, E.A. (1989). US Brands Abroad: An Empirical Study of Global Branding. *International Marketing Review*. Vol. 6. No. 1.

Ryans, Jr., J.K. (1969). Is it Too Soon to Put a Tiger in Every Tank? *Columbia Journal of World Business*, (March-April).

Samiee, S. & Roth, K. (1992). The Influence of Global Marketing Standardization on Performance. *Journal of Marketing*. 56. April.

Sandler, D. M. & Shani, D. (1992). Brand Globally but Advertise Locally?: An Empirical Investigation. *International Marketing Review*. Vol. 9. No. 4.

Siddiqi, M.M.S. (1976). *Planning and Control of Multinational Marketing Strategy: The Issue of Integration*, New York: Arno Press.

Sorenson, R.Z. & Wiechman, U.E. (1975). How Multinationals View Marketing Standardization, *Harvard Business Review*, 53 (May-June), 38.

Terpstra, V. (1967). *American Marketing in the Common Market*, New York: Praeger Special Studies in International Economics and Development.

Tristan, A.D. (1993). Brazil: Franchising Blossoms. *Business Latin America.* September 6.

Wade, J. (1993). Venezuela: Dutch Firm Shakes up Wholesale Sector. *Business Latin America.* January 11.

Walters, P.G.P (1986). International Marketing Policy: A Discussion of the Standardization Construct and its Relevance for Corporate Policy. *Journal of International Business Studies.* Summer.

Wiechman, U.E. (1976). *Marketing Management in Multinational Firms: The Consumer Packaged Goods Industry,* New York: Praeger Publishers.

Wind, Y., Douglas, S.P. and Perlmutter, H.V. (1973). Guidelines for Developing International Marketing Strategies, *Journal of Marketing,* 37 (April), 14-23.

# Advertising to the Masses Without Mass Media: The Case of *Wokabaut* Marketing

Amos Owen Thomas

**SUMMARY.** With media coverage of the interior regions of Papua New Guinea virtually non-existent, an advertising agency has adapted 'live' theatre used previously in development communications to marketing purposes. Considered a local marketing success, it is arguably culturally contextualised. This paper describes the mechanics of this medium and attempts to evaluate its impact. *[Article copies available from The Haworth Document Delivery Service: 1-800-342-9678. E-mail address: getinfo@haworth.com]*

## INTRODUCTION

In this age of global marketing aided by transnational advertising, particularly via television, there are still geographical regions outside the

Amos Owen Thomas is Lecturer in Marketing, School of Business, Monash University, Churchill, Victoria 3842 and is currently researching the advent of transnational television advertising via satellite and cable in Asia. He was previously a lecturer at the Papua New Guinea University of Technology, and prior to that was a copywriting manager with US-owned international advertising agencies based in Singapore, serving multinational clients in the East Asia region.

[Haworth co-indexing entry note]: "Advertising to the Masses Without Mass Media: The Case of *Wokabaut* Marketing." Thomas, Amos Owen. Co-published simultaneously in the *Journal of Global Marketing* (International Business Press, an imprint of The Haworth Press, Inc.) Vol. 9, No. 4, 1996, pp. 75-88; and: *Marketing in the Third World* (ed: Denise M. Johnson, and Erdener Kaynak) International Business Press, an imprint of The Haworth Press, Inc., 1996, pp. 75-88. Single or multiple copies of this article are available from The Haworth Document Delivery Service [1-800-342-9678, 9:00 a.m. - 5:00 p.m. (EST). E-mail address: getinfo@haworth.com].

*75*

reach of modern mass media due, in large part, to lack of economic and technological development. The interior of Papua New Guinea is one such region and Wokabaut Marketing is a local innovation designed to circumvent its media constraints. An urban-based advertising agency has adapted 'live' theatre used previously in development communications to its marketing purposes for the rural interior successfully. This paper describes the mechanics of this medium, and evaluates its cultural contextualisation, socio-economic impact and some ethical implications.

## ORIGIN OF THE CONCEPT

The idea for Wokabaut Marketing (WM) was derived from two disparate sources. The term 'wokabaut' is Pidgin for 'walkabout.' the aboriginal practice of periodic nomadic wandering and one inspiration for WM came from a popular cultural troupe known as the Raun Raun (Pidgin for 'itinerant') Theatre. Funded by the government and based in the Highlands, this professional troupe tours towns and villages in PNG performing tribal songs, dances and skits (Abrams, 1982). Its special blend of elaborate costumes, slapstick humour and audience involvement makes it a very popular, and once the only, form of street entertainment. It also puts on educational plays on family planning, hygiene and other health-related issues. Research on these plays revealed high recall and retention of the educational message (Scott, 1986).

The other inspiration was an importer-distributor who discovered that its instant noodles product had low recognition and usage in the highlands of Papua New Guinea, as the villagers found the written instructions difficult, if not incomprehensible. So in the 1985, a substantial percentage of the advertising media budget was diverted to what the importer described as direct marketing, but would have been more accurately termed sales promotion. A demonstration team visited town centres and large villages, carrying out product education and demonstrations, such as boiling the product. Sales rose significantly, despite the fact that their product was more expensive than its competitors', and that in that year the coffee harvest, the major source of the villagers' cash income, was only average (Bingham, 1987).

Wokabaut Marketing is the brain-child of the managing director of an advertising agency based in Port Moresby, the capital city of Papua New Guinea. It couples the noodle distributor's sales promotion techniques with Raun Raun's entertainment to produce a new advertising medium for the predominantly rural population of this developing country largely unreached by conventional mass media, whether broadcast or print.

## COUNTRY BACKGROUND

### Geography

Papua New Guinea (PNG) lies between the north of Australia and the equator, due east of Indonesia. To its east is the island-dotted region of Oceania on the Pacific Ocean. It comprises the eastern half of the island of New Guinea, the world's second largest, and a number of much smaller islands. The 'mainland' makes up 85% of its territory, the total of which is about the size of Sweden.

The geography of PNG explains some of the cultural diversity and limited socio-economic development of its people. The central spine of the 'mainland' is a mountainous region, called the Highlands, with peaks over 4,000 metres. The terrain restricted movement of its peoples, and resulted in the existence today of over 700 distinct language/tribal groups, many still retaining traditional animosity or, at least, mistrust. 'Tok Pisin' or Pidgin English predominant in the northern half is progressively becoming the lingua franca of the whole country.

The terrain also meant that the Highlands were isolated from the contact with the coast and thus the outside world till the 1930s, when the first Australian explorers ventured in. What was previously thought to be unpopulated, turned out to be the most densely populated region of PNG. Thus only in the past 50-60 years has its stone-age civilisation, by 'western' standards, slowly encountered the industrial age. The country gained independence from Australia, its UN mandated administrators, only in 1975.

### Economy

The relatively nascent PNG economy is largely subsistence agriculture, resource-based, high-cost, aid-dependent and public sector dominated (Millett 1990). Recent statistics indicate that about 50% of the population 10 years and above, were involved in farming or fishing, and only 10% had a wage job. Highlanders have additional income from cash-cropping of coffee and cocoa. The average per capita income in PNG is US$928 (World Economic Data, 1991).

Though the world's largest copper mine in the province of Bouganville is still closed due to a secessionist rebellion, discoveries of gold, silver and oil made in the late 1980s are beginning to come onstream. PNG is expected to be the 6th largest gold-producing nation. According to World Bank estimates, government revenues from minerals are expected to top US$751 million in 1993. Agriculture, forestry and fishery resources are largely untapped. Thus, in comparison to other developing countries, PNG has much potential for economic development, if it overcomes a growing breakdown of law-and-order, due in part to the disparity of modern and traditional cultures, roughly divided into the urban 'haves' and rural 'have-nots.'

## *Marketing*

The practice of professional marketing is embryonic in Papua New Guinea. As in many third-world countries, it is generally a seller's market, given the limited range of manufactured goods available for consumption and minimal competition between brands. It is often seen as a distribution outpost for Australian manufacturers and marketers, occasionally a dumping ground for failed products elsewhere. Marketing information is scarce and proprietary to the marketers, though most of this is inference about purchasing behaviour from sales figures (Farbood, 1990). The transition from a traditional exchange to a modern marketing system in the rural regions of PNG could take years, even decades. Meanwhile innovative marketing systems adapted to the socio-cultural environment, such as Wokabaut Marketing, seem the basis for business success today and possibly a foundation for future developments.

The primary channel for retailing is via the ubiquitous trade stores, a number existing side by side in more populated areas, or a single one per village in more sparsely populated ones. Typical of other developing countries (see Hussein, 1989; Blois, 1991), these stores are family-owned and sell a small range of staple, manufactured and packaged goods, such as canned fish, corned beef, rice, crackers, instant coffee, milk powder, detergent, etc., to a small consumer catchment area. In small towns along the highways, larger or wholesale stores sell in bulk mostly to trade stores, though occasionally to large family groups.

## *Mass Media*

The mass media of PNG comprises 3 newspapers, 2 national radio networks and 1 commercial TV station. Only one newspaper is a daily, published on weekdays, and is in English. With a circulation of 33,900 and a pass-on rate averaging 5.0, the *Post-Courier* has a total readership of 169,500, less than 5% of the population of 3.9 million. The two other papers are weeklies: The *Times* of PNG, also in English, with an audited circulation of 13,000 with an estimated pass-on rate of 3-4, and *Wantok*, in Pidgin, with a circulation of 15,000 with an estimated pass-on rate of 9-11 (UN, 1992).

Of the two national radio networks, one is Radio Karai–the government station which does not accept advertising. The other is Radio Kalang an FM station, also owned by the government but run as a commercial network. Its potential listenership is estimated at 1.5 million or 83% of the population of major semi-urban areas (First Market Search, 1988). Local radio stations, owned by provincial governments and broadcasting in the major dialects of the area, do not accept advertising.

Television is the most recent entrant to the media scene. EMTV, a subsidiary of Australia's Channel Nine network, is the sole survivor of the two stations that entered PNG in 1987. It has a potential viewership estimated at 300,000 (Taylor, 1990). It is transmitted by microwave to urban centres, mostly provincial capitals around which electricity is available. Statistics are lacking but there is believed to be a high overlap of newspaper and TV audiences. There are plans by the telecommunications authority to extend TV reception to rural areas by the mid-1990s through the use of satellite transmission.

## MECHANICS OF WOKABAUT MARKETING

### Schedule and Reach

Wokabaut Marketing (WM) now has 2 troupes which tour most of the Highlands and part of the northern coast of New Guinea Island, covering 6 provinces in all which account for 57% of the country's population. Each province is visited for a total of 4.5 weeks during the 12 separate tours undertaken annually by the troupes.

About 15 locations are visited on each troupe's tour lasting 3 weeks with some repetition of location over the course of the year to reinforce learning. The troupes tend to perform in town centres, high schools, urban squatter settlements, villages and markets, maintaining a ratio of two rural areas to each semi-urban one. Schools, usually found in or near small towns, are targeted as places predisposed to behaviour modification and their students as catalysts of change upon return to their villages. The troupe also performs at major tribal shows in the various towns, which draw thousands of visitors from the neighbouring regions. The total audience in the first year of operations was estimated at 252,000 (Wiley 1990), making it a quasi-mass media. Since there is an unspecified degree of repeated visits per site, its reach may not be quite comparable to that of broadcast and print media. Nonetheless WM does reach an audience which is unreachable otherwise by the mass media.

Each troupe has a separate client list of about half-a-dozen clients whose products are non-competitive. The advertising agency has a policy of marketing only products which they claim benefit the villagers and do not adversely affect their lifestyle. A client list included biscuits, toiletries, pharmaceutical products, rice, canned corned beef, coffee, chewing gum, automobiles,[1] rubber boots, paints, insect repellents and tools. It declines tobacco and liquor products, both of which are popular in this market and actively marketed using point-of-sale or non-media promotion. As these products are recognised sources of health and social problems, there are some legal constraints on their advertising in other mass media in the country as well.

### Production and Performance

To each product is devoted a one-act play, which functions as a 'live' commercial. A draft script by the client is then modified and elaborated upon by the troupe in the field under the supervision of a director. A videotaped rehearsal is sent back to the client for approval before the play is performed publicly. Each client may advertise a maximum of 3 products for about US$24,000 per year, payment being in two 6-monthly install-ments. This is comparable to the cost of 600 radio spots, or 84 non-prime spots on the sole television station.

As a rule the troupe arrives unannounced by truck at a location such as a village square, drawing a crowd ranging from 300 to 1,500 on-lookers, some curious but many now familiar with what to expect. The troupe proceeds to set up a make-shift plywood backdrop on the truck which serves as the stage. Rock music plays from a tape-deck as preparations are made 'back stage' of the truck. The actors are equipped with wireless microphones for easy mobility on stage and audibility by the audience scattered about the vicinity, and the language used is Pidgin, the 'lingua franca' of northern Papua New Guinea.

A sampling of the plots of the one-act plays includes a reluctant child being taught how to brush his teeth with toothpaste, a husband's bungled attempts to swat a fly and later learning to use an aerosol can properly, a mother explaining ways to cook canned-fish, or a picnic of young people using crackers and rice-cakes. All of this done in an indigenous brand of slapstick humour, the Wokabaut troupe has the rapt attention, gleeful laughter and even active participation of an audience that has little access to alternative entertainment.

Often at the end of each act free samples of the product or discount coupons are distributed. Wokabaut coupons redeemable at wholesalers or retailers are one measure of effectiveness of the medium. A chain of stores which participated in such a scheme experienced 95% redemption despite it involving the consumers travelling from their village to the store in town and trying a new product (Bingham, 1987). It is doubtful whether the coupons would have succeeded without the promotional communication by the Wokabaut troupe. The troupe also assists in setting up point-of-sale promotional materials at trade-stores en route. At nightfall, after the performance, the troupe puts on videotaped TV programmes to continue the entertainment and to reinforce the commercial message through advertisements specially edited into the programmes.

## CRITIQUE OF THE MEDIUM

### Social Responsibility

Wokabaut Marketing claims to be filling a gap in the geographic and demographic reach of the local mass media. But it is worth noting, by contrast, that Indonesia banned TV advertising in 1981 for fear of it causing social unrest in rural areas with low purchasing power (Napis and Roth, 1982), although that decision has since been revoked. A similar situation to Indonesia's a decade ago still exists today in the rural highlands and coastal regions of PNG, where the purchase of products promoted by WM would represent a disproportionate share of the consumer's cash income. It is reasonably well-documented that low-income consumers in third-world countries are persuaded by marketers to spend on advertised products what is needed for more basic necessities (Medawar, 1979).

Average spending by urban consumers of Papua New Guinea (nationals, as opposed to expatriates) is estimated by retail marketers at US $30 per household per week. No figures exist for the rural population but it would be considerably less. Thus it is probably premature for the promotion of consumer goods to be directed at these rural poor in addition to the urban elite already reached by the mass media. There already exists a drift of rural people to the urban areas, with towns and cities facing an estimated growth rate of 10% per year. Ending up unemployed and living in shantytowns, these people are alleged to be partly responsible for the breakdown of law-and-order in urban areas. This is because it is widely believed that they seek to fulfil their consumer wants and needs, denied them by legitimate economic means, through crime. Therefore, marketing techniques and advertising media which reach pre-modern interior regions of the country, are frequently cited by social and political leaders in Papua New Guinea as contributory factors to this social problem, regardless of whether such as relationship can be demonstrated by research.

Commendable as the advertising agency's policy on tobacco and liquor may be, it is debatable whether some of the products promoted meet its own criterion of having no adverse effect on lifestyles. Much of the rural population subsists on sweet potatoes, yams and vegetables, supplementing it only occasionally with meat, canned or fresh. Even for those whose regular purchases might already include canned-fish, imported rice and sugar, the promotion of potato crisps, house-paint and chewing gum is questionable, especially when more basic human needs for nutrition, health-care, clean water, education and electricity remain unmet. As van Ginneken and Baron (1984) found in a number of case-studies, preference for modern over traditional products among low-income consumers in developing countries may have as much to with superior marketing techniques as with benefits of product quality to the consumer through better production technology.

### *Cultural Contextualisation*

Although WM aims to provide a indigenous or at least culturally-sensitive medium of marketing communications, on analysis much of it is of a foreign culture and technology. An itinerant drama troupe has no equivalent in traditional PNG culture, the closest thing to which being the practice of story-telling by tribal or village elders. The troupe arrives by truck, often in villages barely accessible to the few other vehicles that come their way. They set up a stage backdrop that resembles an urban house of non-indigenous or quasi-'western' design. They use an amplifier and speakers to play disco music, which is quite foreign to the majority of the rural audience, as an overture to the performance.

The plays have a recurrent though latent theme of emulating one's urban 'westernised' counterparts in the use of products. The TV sets left on at night, powered by the troupe's generators, bring into the village, via the programmes and advertising, a depiction of a lifestyle beyond their means. Over 70% of these programmes, taped off the sole local TV station, are of foreign, mostly U.S., origin and comprise a high proportion of soap-operas, sitcoms, police-dramas and westerns (Thomas, 1994). In addition the draft script for the troupe's acts are written by the client represented by an expatriate, usually Australian, executive. Then it is sent to the troupe, comprising PNG nationals, who provide the relevant local input. But they are supervised by another expatriate (at one time an Italian designer), a fact that the advertising agency stresses in its marketing to largely expatriate clients (Wiley, 1990).

What Anderson (1984) said of the expatriate domination of advertising in the well-established Southeast Asian marketplace, seems no less true in the less-developed South Pacific today. Foreign-made advertising materials are banned in PNG on the grounds that they would be culturally inappropriate and insensitive. While that is true, to a certain extent such legislation serves only to ensure that nationals, both urban and rural, are more effectively persuaded. This is because the advertising is culturally contextualised and thus better able to bridge the gap between the sellers' and buyers' cultures. Nonetheless it is created by locally-experienced expatriate specialists rather than by PNG nationals. In addition, this regulation facilitates the oligopoly within the local economy of predominantly foreign-owned and managed advertising agencies acting for the similarly owned and managed importer-distributors of the products of multinational corporations.

Most developed countries have legislated or at least its citizen groups have lobbied for industry self-regulation on advertising to children. It is well-researched and long recognised there that young children are not able to discern the selling intent of TV advertising (Federal Trade Commission, 1978). Thus it might be reasonable to assume that content of the message approximates effect as the audience lacks the socio-cultural sophistication with which to filter the persuasive message. In a less-developed country, this argument might arguably be extended to teenagers and adults of limited or no formal education who also lack urban socialisation and access to alternative sources of consumer information. While it might be argued that all PNG nationals have the right to receive whatever promotional messages they choose, the pivotal issue here is the very selective exposure that the rural poor have at the present time, often solely via WM since they do not have ready access to print or broadcast media.

Through advertising only non-competitive products in rural, interior regions where there is little or no other advertising, WM is able to achieve strong brand loyalty by influencing consumers there to associate a product category with a particular brand. James (1983) would argue that such unbalanced promotion tends to cause greater spending on new products which have no inherent advantage over their more traditional substitutes. Therefore it can hardly be said to be paternalistic for a developing country such as PNG to have social policies designed to modify the perceived utility of manufactured goods, and this might be communicated sensitively without implying gullibility on the part of its rural citizens.

## Medium as Message

Other mass media which offer advertising provide informational and/or entertainment programming of a non-commercial nature to its audience as well. Advertising usually occupies a very minor proportion of the time or space in the medium, a proportion often regulated by the government. The medium's audience has the option of whether to pay attention to the advertising inserted into the programming or to ignore, even walk away from it. Wokabaut Marketing has succeeded in devising a medium that is unadulterated advertising, even if educational and entertaining in character. The audience does not have the option of selective attention, and may not have a choice in watching the entire performance as it is quite intrusive into the life of the village or rural marketplace.

Most advertisers have to purchase time or space on a medium in which to convey its message. Once the villagers realise this to be the practice, WM may be confronted with their 'compensation' demands for the use of the physical space.[2] For the present, there appears to be no attempt at seeking permission from the village leaders to perform, since surprise is a crucial element of this medium. There is the likely future scenario of competitors adopting similar or identical direct marketing methods. In that eventuality every village may be subject to not just 1-2 visits from each WM troupe per year, but some multiple of that figure. Quite possibly the audiences would decline in number or attentiveness, and the reception from the tribal leadership could be less enthusiastic, even hostile.

## MARKETING AND DEVELOPMENT

### Socio-Cultural Change

Wokabaut Marketing is certainly accelerating the diffusion of consumer goods into the rural regions to the benefit of its sponsors, though its role in bringing about social change to interior PNG is unclear. For one thing, the promotion of manufactured goods can undermine a social structure and culture in PNG where reciprocal gift-giving of primary produce is an essential element of social integration. Arnould (1989) documents a similar development in Niger where previously gifts were the produce of their own lands, but the substitution of consumer goods in symbolic exchange has placed great pressure on the possession of cash in a traditional subsistence economy.

Diffusion of consumer goods and attendant cultural practices to rural villages through migrant workers returning from urban areas does take place in PNG, but this is a slower process without high-pressure promotion by marketers. It suffers less from the acute demand for cash experienced in the rural subsistence economy, as the goods are paid for from wages earned in an urban cash economy by those migrant workers. Further, they make their choices as more sophisticated consumers who would have had protracted exposure to the competitive marketplace of products during their urban sojourn.

The social and cultural consequences of marketing, more difficult to research than the economic especially in developing countries, may be more far-reaching. WM, like all advertising, works psychologically to change attitudes, values, cognitions, etc., in promoting consumption. Instead of reflecting the indigenous culture, advertising such as Wokabaut Marketing reinforces certain elements of the culture that favour consumption, such as materialism and individualism, acting as a 'distorted mirror' (Pollay, 1988). This may account partially for the postulated gradual erosion of the strong kinship and communalism characteristic of tribal PNG society.

### *Politico-Economic Change*

Advertising is often seen as a necessary correlate of economic development, helping to increase consumption, and thus production and market growth. Kaynak (1989) believes that advertising, by promoting a higher standard of living, is a positive force in modernisation and development even if it is somewhat distrusted by Third World governments. Advertising in developing countries can play an educational as well as a persuasive role, with the distinction usually blurred as in the case with WM. But Kaynak also recognises that advertising has differing impacts on individuals in different countries due to varying stages of their socio-economic development and cultural background.

The economic benefit of any marketing activity to a developing nation is doubtful if it promotes goods that are foreign-made, for instance PNG where advertising does little to stimulate investment and job-creation. Furthermore, research by Callahan (1985) suggests that advertising is not significantly related to economic development but merely changes the composition of consumption as manufacturers use it to compete for their share of the market. Surveying a number of other studies, he concludes that advertising expenditure in national markets is dependent on past consumption rather than the other way around.

Joy and Ross (1989) evaluate various attempts to bridge the gaps in our understanding of the links between marketing and economic development in the context of developing countries. Rejecting the modernisation school for its uni-dimensional approach, and the institutional school for its ahistoricity, they favour a revision of the radical school with its emphasis on the capitalist world-system. Among other things this view advocates marketing strategies based on thorough historical and cultural analysis, recognition of enduring local institutions, and value-judgements on real needs of various substrata of society. Wokabaut Marketing appears not to practise these principles of partnership in economic development which Joy and Ross consider essential to long-term marketing success.

## CONCLUSIONS

Governments of developing countries periodically express concern about the social impact of marketing and tend to focus on the activities of large multinational corporations. Yet the impact of such marketing may be no less, and be probably greater, through the efforts of indigenous forms of promotion such as Wokabaut Marketing on behalf of global manufacturers. While being remarkably effective, because they are low-key such marketing activities tend to escape the notice of policy-makers. However, professional marketing which is in tune with a nation's socio-cultural context and meets real needs of specific regions within it might succeed in the long-run and could be an effective partner in its economic development.

Much as it is needed, there is a dearth of empirical research on the long-term impact of various marketing practices in PNG as in other developing countries, particularly their more remote regions. This is due in no small measure to the logistical difficulties of access to remote villages, the socio-cultural constraints of conducting surveys or focus groups among a largely illiterate and premodern communities unfamiliar with such techniques, and thus the relative high cost vis-à-vis benefit of such activity for these markets (see Tuncalp, 1988). The situation will not change so long as countries like Papua New Guinea are seen as of marginal import to market and academic researchers alike.

The critical issue which this case raises is whether markets for manufactured consumer goods should be extended into rural subsistence economies ahead of economic development programmes. In the view of this author, perhaps this ought to be a matter of social enquiry leading to national concensus and economic planning coordinated by the governments of developing countries, rather than an independent decision of commercial organisations largely directed by transnational interests.

## NOTES

1. Automobiles may seem a strange inclusion for a target market of low-income, unless one bears in mind that such products are purchased and utilised on an extended-family or clan basis. Some cars are used on the dirt tracks leading to remote villages and invariably have a short life-span.

2. Land compensation demands characterise many modern developments in PNG, such as road construction and mining. Petty claims for compensation for any form of intrusion or injury are a common characteristic of the local culture.

## REFERENCES

Abrams, Tevia (1989),"Papua New Guinea strives to strengthen its traditional communication system: highlights of a 1980 Unesco report," *Folk media and mass media in population communication*. Paris: Unesco.

Anderson, Michael H. (1984), *Madison Avenue in Asia: politics and trans-national advertising*, London: Associated Universities Presses.

Arnould, Eric J. (1989), "Towards a broadened theory of preference formation and the diffusion of innovation: cases from Zinder Province, Niger Republic," *Journal of Consumer Research*, 16.

Bingham, Clara (1987) "Consumerism comes to the bush," *Asian Advertising and Marketing*. (Feb.), pp. 16-19, 28.

Blois, K. J. (1989), "Supermarkets and their role in Chinese retailing," *European Journal of Marketing*, 23, (3).

Callahan, Francis X. (1985), "Advertising and economic development," *Media Asia*, 12 (3).

Farbood, Ali (1990), "Marketing and its role in the development of Papua New Guinea" (Unpublished working paper). Lae: Department of Business Studies, PNG University of Technology.

Federal Trade Commission (1978), *FTC Staff Report On Television Advertising to Children*, Washington.

Hussein, R. T. (1991), "Personal values and food retail store choice: the case of Jordan," *Journal of International Marketing and Marketing Research*, 15 (1).

James, Jeffrey (1983), *Consumer choice in the Third World: a study of welfare effects of advertising and new products in a developing country*, London: MacMillan Press.

Joy, Annama and Christopher A. Ross (1989), "Marketing and development in Third World contexts: an evaluation and future directions," *Journal of Macromarketing*, (Fall).

Kaynak, Erdener (1989) "Advertising and development" (chapter 6), *The management of international advertising*, New York: Quorum Books.

Levitt, Theodore (1983), "The globalisation of markets," *Harvard Business Review*, (May-June).

Medawar, Charles (1979), *Insult or injury: an enquiry into the marketing and advertising of British food and drug products in the Third World*, London: Social Audit Ltd., 53-55.

Millett, John (1990), *Private sector development in Papua New Guinea* (Discussion Paper No. 42), Port Moresby: Institute of National Affairs.

Napis, M. and Roth, R.N. (1982), "Advertising in Indonesia," *International Advertiser*, 3, (3), (Nov.), 12.

Pollay, Richard (1988), "Advertising and cultural change: problems with the propaganda for progress," *International Conference on Marketing and Development*, Budapest, (July).

Scott, David C. (1986), "On the jungle road with Colgate toothpaste," *Christian Science Monitor*, (Jan. 9), 6.

Taylor, John (1990), Interview in Sept of the managing director of EMTV.

Thomas, Amos Owen (1994) "Broadcast policy versus commercial imperative: television programming in Papua New Guinea." *Media Asia*, 21, (1).

Tuncalp, Secil (1988), "The marketing research scene in Saudi Arabia," *European Journal of Marketing*, 22, (5).

United Nations (1992), *World Media Handbook*, New York: United Nations Dept. of Public Information.

van Ginneken, Wouter and Christopher Baron (1984), *Appropriate products, employment and technology*, London: MacMillan Press.

Ward, Scott (1974), "Consumer socialization," *Journal of Consumer Research*, 1, (September).

Wiley, Chris (1990), *Wokabaut Marketing Proposal*, Port Moresby, Papua New Guinea: HRD Advertising, (March).

*World Economic Data* (1991), Third Edition, Santa Barbara: ABC-CLIO.

# A Framework
## for Effective Global Marketing
## for Developing
## Country Public Sector Enterprises

Erdener Kaynak
Ali Kara

**SUMMARY.** Public sector organizations show distinct differences in structure, management, philosophy, and performance when compared to private sector organizations. In recent years, however, public sector organizations have emerged as important income contributors and a potent technology source to developing countries through their active internationalization efforts. Public sector organizations have begun to enter and operate in international markets, due to the home-country push and host-country pull factors. The purpose of this conceptual paper is to examine the globalization process of developing country public sector enterprises and develop a marketing oriented framework for effective internationalization process. *[Article copies available from The Haworth Document Delivery Service: 1-800-342-9678. E-mail address: getinfo@haworth.com]*

Erdener Kaynak is Professor of Marketing, School of Business Administration, Pennsylvania State University at Harrisburg, Middletown, PA 17057. Ali Kara is Assistant Professor of Business Administration, College of Business Administration, Pennsylvania State University at York, York, PA 17403.

[Haworth co-indexing entry note]: "A Framework for Effective Global Marketing for Developing Country Public Sector Enterprises." Kaynak, Erdener, and Ali Kara. Co-published simultaneously in the *Journal of Global Marketing* (International Business Press, an imprint of The Haworth Press, Inc.) Vol. 9, No. 4, 1996, pp. 89-108; and: *Marketing in the Third World* (ed: Denise M. Johnson, and Erdener Kaynak) International Business Press, an imprint of The Haworth Press, Inc., 1996, pp. 89-108. Single or multiple copies of this article are available from The Haworth Document Delivery Service [1-800-342-9678, 9:00 a.m. - 5:00 p.m. (EST). E-mail address: getinfo@haworth.com].

## INTRODUCTION

Traditionally, public sector firms were confined to public utilities such as energy, transportation, communications, iron, steel, and coal production and most of their activities were directed to the domestic markets. Public-sector enterprises are organized as corporations, companies, boards, statutory agencies, and autonomous bodies whose functions range from agriculture, manufacturing, mining and extractive activities, trading, and marketing (Premchand 1979). Generally, they are owned and/or controlled by governments and/or government agencies. They are usually autonomously organized with the government providing the initial capital and then monitoring the activities in a constant manner.

Public-sector enterprises have significant share in manufacturing and trade in the world. They produce 85 percent of the world's oil, 40 percent of its copper, and 33 percent of its iron ore and bauxite. In the manufacturing sector, they produce 54 percent of the steel, 35 percent of the polyethylene, and 20 percent of autos. Generally, public enterprises remain relatively insignificant in the areas of consumer goods, food processing, and furniture production, which are usually left to the private sector. These figures are more dramatic for developing countries. For instance, public enterprises contribute about 40 percent of the GDP in Bolivia, 25 percent in Pakistan, and about 16 percent in India. In terms of industries, the public sector owns all (or nearly all) of the postal service, telecommunications, electricity, gas, oil production, coal, and railways in such developing countries as Brazil, India, and Mexico, and the postal service and railways in South Korea and Spain. In both India and Spain, airlines are also publicly owned. Public sector organizations have also spread beyond traditional areas into virtually all economic sectors, including manufacturing, construction, services, agriculture, and natural resources. These enterprises now account for 75 percent of industrial value added in Egypt, 60 percent in Bangladesh, 33 percent in Nepal and Sri Lanka, 20 percent in India, and 16.5 percent in South Korea (Gillis and Peprah 1981-82).

Furthermore, in countries such as Mexico, Brazil, and India, where public-sector enterprises have a dominant role, the largest industrial company is publicly owned. In particular, the three largest Brazilian enterprises in terms of assets are state owned, as are two of the three largest Mexican enterprises and the nine largest domestic firms in Indonesia. In terms of sales, on the other hand, twelve of the sixteen largest Korean enterprises are state owned (Gillis and Peprah 1981-82).

Over the past several years, pressure for globalization began to develop rapidly and public-sector enterprises now play a more important role in global markets, relative to their domestic operations (Cornell 1993; Treheux 1992; Papathanassopoulos 1990). As such, they are emerging as a significant competitive force in some principal areas such as (a) extractive industries–mineral, petroleum, copper, and iron, (b) manufacturing–automobiles, petrochemicals, and metals, and (c) in some service industries (Rhodes 1979).

Hence, the purpose of this paper is to examine the internationalization process of developing country public-sector enterprises and develop a marketing oriented framework for effective internationalization process. In particular, public sector organizations' entry and operational methods are analyzed in addition to their organizational behavior and strategy formulation while operating in a variety of foreign markets.

## GENERAL CHARACTERISTICS OF PSEs

There are four major types of enterprise organizations found in developing countries: (a) the entrepreneurial firm, (b) the industrial cluster, (c) the multinational subsidiary, and (d) the public-sector enterprise. It is stated by Jorgensen et al. (1986) that the public enterprise is one component of a divisionalized organization, in which the divisions report to the cabinet as the ultimate board of directors. The relationship between market imperfections and the structure of public-sector enterprise is charted in Figure 1.

In a planned developing economy, the state assumes a variety of functions to organize and direct the production and distribution of goods and services, both domestically and internationally. The state can exercise both direct and indirect control over the main market forces such as demand, supply, prices, and conditions of sale. Organizationally, the marketing activities of public enterprises are distributed among three levels of management–namely strategic, managerial, and operative (see Table 1).

At the strategic level of the organization, there are those general national bodies such as State Planning Organization, State Statistics Institute and the relevant ministry (i.e., Ministry of Trade, Industry, or Food and Agriculture, etc.). At this level, marketing activities are performed in line with the national economic goals as well as in accordance with priorities of five-year economic development plans as well as yearly programs (Zavialov and Abramishvili 1982). Whereas, at the managerial level, there are different ministries such as defense, food and agriculture, and industry and trade, which also serve as headquarters for a variety of industries. There are a multitude of industrial enterprises in each industry. Through these industrial enterprises, national economic goals are translated into specific products. In order to create the products and services demanded by citizens and also meet foreign currency needs, ministries allocate the neces-

FIGURE 1. Public-Sector Enterprises with Divisionalized Organizational Structure

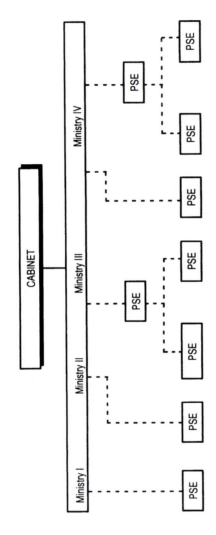

**Key Market Imperfections**

- Lack of competition
- General supply imperfections
- Managerial and board turnover unrelated to economic performance
- Shortage of managerial talent

**Consequences**

- Bloated inventories, hoarding and bargaining
- Goal displacement
- Emphasis on political survival rather than effectiveness or efficiency
- Skilled personnel allowed to engage in outside business

Source: adapted from Jorgensen, Hafsi and Kiggundu (1986), pp. 428 & 429.

TABLE 1. Organization of Marketing Activities by Public Enterprises During Internationalization

| Different Levels | Decision Making Units and Activities | | |
|---|---|---|---|
| STRATEGIC | State Planning Agency | State Statistics Institute | Related Ministries |
| MANAGERIAL | Enterprise I | Enterprise II | Enterprise III |
| OPERATIVE | Marketing of Goods to Country A | Marketing of Goods to Country B | Marketing of Goods to Country C |
| ACTIVITIES PERFORMED | Setting up organizational structures, development of marketing strategies, and establishing relations with distributors and customers overseas. | | |

Source: Adapted from Zavialov and Abramishvili 1982, p. 206.

sary resources among various enterprises on the basis of state planning agency allocations. Finally, at the operational level, industrial and commercial enterprises being organized and directed by higher levels of state bureaucratic management, prepare action programs where strategic marketing plans, organizational structures, and manufacturing and sourcing plans, as well as the establishment of sales and delivery services, are developed and implemented. At times, there may be a divergence between short-term micro-economic objectives of a public-sector enterprise and long-term macroeconomic targets of the Central Planning Authority or the ministry concerned.

When the performance of public enterprises in international markets are analyzed, it is obvious that there is a less than satisfactory performance. They are, in most cases, less efficient than their counterparts in the private sector. This unsatisfactory performance may result from their high production costs because of the non-commercial objectives maintained by public enterprises, price controls on inputs and outputs, and poor financial structure of the enterprise. It is also the result of poor management practices that continue to employ unsuitable production patterns and outdated technology, which results in low labor productivity, and poor marketing. Managers of public enterprises often also lack adequate experience in running commercially viable enterprises. These managers also lack clear performance objectives, and they do not receive incentives for better performance.

## THE GLOBALIZATION PROCESS OF PSEs

There has been ever increasing demand in developing countries for foreign currency in order to finance their socio-economic and technological development efforts. Mazzolini (1980) proposed that three sets of pressures on the internationalization of public-sector enterprises exist. These are hindrances to foreign expansion, pressures for particular patterns of organizational behavior and international marketing strategy.

In key sectors such as steel, raw materials, and petrochemicals, most of the production and marketing activity is carried out domestically due to the desire to maintain direct control. Foreign marketing activity is considered only when there is a surplus product. In most of the developing countries, governments are interested in developing the economies in the less-developed areas of their country. In these cases, public enterprises are forced to invest more in certain areas of their domestic markets and invest less in markets abroad. Hence, public sector enterprises assumed to be responsible with sustaining their national economy cannot be expected to be aggressive in international markets. Some developing-country governments have negative attitudes toward foreign expansion of public sector firms because they assume that it would negatively affect their countries' balance of payments and employment. In some other countries, conservative government officials feel that public enterprises ought not to be allowed to grow because growth is considered as losing control over the operation of the public sector enterprises. Since international expansion is considered as a growth opportunity for the public sector companies, governments forced them to stay at domestic markets (Mazzolini 1980).

Besides the above mentioned hindrances to foreign expansion of public-sector enterprises, there are certain driving forces for foreign expansion. For instance, when a developing country does not possess natural resources of its own in certain strategic sectors, the domestic government exerts pressure on the appropriate public sectors to become involved in the extraction of the needed resources from international markets. At times, some of the public enterprises from Eastern Block countries are asked to make certain investments in countries considered friendly within the context of their domestic government's foreign-policy guidelines. One also witnesses such political pressures in service industries as banking, shipping, insurance, and airlines. For example, airlines are asked to operate certain unprofitable routes. Heenan (1981) summarizes the reasons for public-sector enterprises' expansion into foreign markets in three categories: (1) obtaining hard currency, (2) fulfilling their political aims, and (3) gathering intelligence.

On the other hand, a transition from central planning to free-market economy through decentralization and deregulation occurs in the internationalization process of public-sector enterprises. Public enterprises perform differently from private enterprises at each stage because of the varying degrees of state control or government influence. Nelson (1982) identifies five clusters of countries with distinct characteristics clarifying the role and operation of public enterprises (see Figure 2).

The first group of countries includes South Korea, Togo, Nigeria, and Turkey. In these countries, the private industry and Western liberal ideology dominate. In Korea, for instance, the building industry is independent, but is financed by the government. Many enterprises are mixed (public/private) in these countries, and cooperate with foreign firms. In particular, public-sector enterprises enter into joint ventures with multinationals, particularly in the natural-resources area.

The second group of countries are those demonstrating a clear capitalist profile, but whose public enterprises play a dominant role. For instance, Pakistan and Brazil have established very large public enterprises in their basic industries. Governments in these countries increasingly favor arrangements wherein the state itself, through one of its public-sector enterprises, is the joint venture partner. Recent examples include mining projects in Brazil, and fishery projects in Indonesia.

The third category is comprised of those countries having reasonable amounts of experience with socialist economic systems where state-owned and controlled enterprises dominated in all fields. There has been a move toward denationalization (privatization) in some developing country industries where there was a lack of production and under-utilization of the country's resources along with inefficient operation (Ackerman 1994).

In the fourth category, those developing countries with socialist orientation, where there is a state control over the economy, are grouped. The public-sector enterprises in these countries are dependent on the orders from other public-sector enterprises. Foreign firms are encouraged to form joint ventures with the public-sector enterprises.

Finally, in the last category, public-sector enterprises are isolated and the whole economy is controlled completely by the government.

## INTERNATIONAL MARKETING POLICIES AND STRATEGIES FOR PSEs

Although most developing-country public enterprises are domestic-market based and are oriented toward meeting the needs of their home markets, they have also need policies and programs for international markets (Beveridge 1995; Snavely 1991). As a result of home-based push and

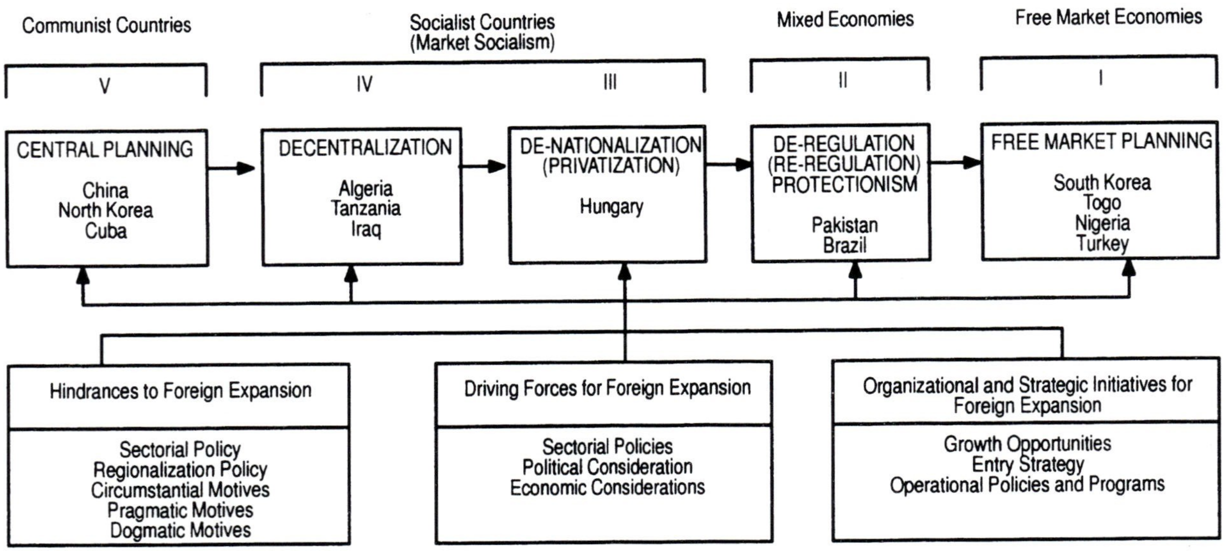

FIGURE 2. Globalization of Public Sector Enterprises from Developing Countries

foreign-country pull forces, developing-country public enterprises started exploring foreign market opportunities (Alexander 1994). However, increased competition in international markets has necessitated more sophisticated marketing management approaches. The level of sophistication is determined by the level of involvement in international marketing. Levels of public enterprise involvement in international marketing can be established by relating them to levels of involvement in international business (Johansson and Vahlne 1975), or as phases of internationalization of the enterprise (Soldner 1977). In light of this conceptual framework, one can develop a construct for the analysis of international marketing management of public sector enterprises ranging from export marketing as an initial entry strategy (Cavusgil and Nevin 1980) to transnational marketing (Robinson 1978) with foreign marketing (Terpstra 1983, p. 157) and multinational marketing (Wiechmann 1974) stages as intermediate steps (see Figure 3).

The first stage in the international marketing process is *export marketing*, whereby public enterprises are entirely national (domestic based) in their nature and scope, marketing varying percentages of their output (up to 10 percent) to overseas markets, either directly or through intermediaries. The second stage is *foreign marketing*, where public-sector enterprises are predominately national, and service important markets through their own sales subsidiaries.

Research indicates that there are several factors affecting public sector enterprises successes in global markets. Poor knowledge of potential markets, lack of ability to follow-up on trade leads, lack of a mechanism to generate trade leads, lack of skilled personnel for export planning and implementation and national (domestic) habits and focus (Naidu and Rao 1993; Treheux 1992). Thus, designing marketing programs for the many national markets is the task of the international marketing manager of the public-sector enterprise. This involves the coordination and integration of the many different national programs into an effective, synergistic, *multinational marketing* activity. *Transnational marketing* deals with the global business entities that exploit world market opportunities by utilizing global resources to transnational market segments. These transnational market segments are established on the basis of geographically adjacent countries. This kind of comparative marketing analysis leads to truly transnational market clusters showing similar traits as to marketing goals, functions and techniques, and instruments which facilitate the international marketing process (Kaynak 1984).

FIGURE 3. Global Marketing Orientation of Public Sector Enterprises

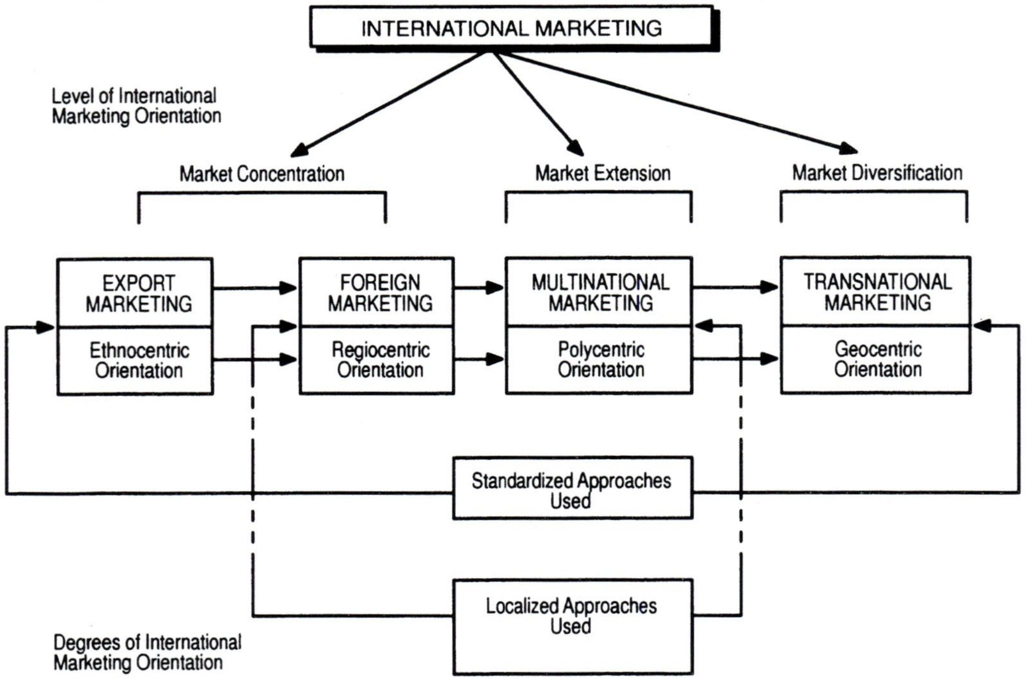

Source: Adapted from Erdener Kaynak, *International Marketing Management*, Praeger Special Studies, New York, 1984, p. 5.

## Market Growth Opportunities in Global Markets

Currently, the role of public-sector enterprises in overseas markets is much smaller than their domestic operation. Generally, these enterprises have more overseas investment in raw materials, infrastructure, and service sectors than in manufacturing. For instance, half of Argentinean public-sector foreign ventures in the electricity, gas, and extractive sectors, whereas their distinct competency in the home market lies in a number of manufacturing industries such as petrochemicals, shipbuilding, steel, and metalworking (White 1983, p. 61). Furthermore, in terms of market orientation of public-sector enterprises, most of these enterprises are local or regional oriented. As such there is a clear intra-regional concentration, and one can very seldom see global, multinational marketing approaches.

On the other hand, it is argued in this paper that public-sector enterprises possess certain distinct competitive advantages in their internationalization efforts. The most important advantage is the lower costs of labor, supplies, and materials. For instance, a Korean public enterprise bidding on a construction contract in the Middle East, or an Indian company involved in manufacturing in Malaysia has a distinct competitive advantage over private companies. An additional advantage is the appropriateness of their labor intensive technologies. It is more suitable for markets where there is high unemployment and minimum maintenance capabilities. Consequently, their knowledge of market conditions in developing countries is a plus. Finally, developing-country public-sector enterprises are more welcomed by the receiving developing countries because they come from weaker countries and they may be perceived to pose little threat to political or economic independence of the host country (Connolly 1984).

Badran and Hinings (1981) state that the key catalysts for change of public-sector enterprises are growth, technology, financial autonomy, and internationalization. Because of market growth opportunities, more public-sector enterprises are expanding their operations to overseas markets. Despite this interest in overseas markets by public-sector enterprises of developing countries, their performance has not been spectacular. A number of reasons can be listed for their less than satisfactory performance in international markets. First, these enterprises generally have domestic orientation (enthnocentric) which is traditionally introspective. As such, they are involved in international marketing in a passive way only. Because of close and frequent association with the military sector, their overseas ventures are often considered a matter of national security. Second, in most cases, public enterprises operate under monopolistic conditions in their domestic markets. This established business practice in the domestic market makes them reluctant and unexperienced in the competitive overseas environment. Finally, because most of these enterprises develop a prevailing risk averse attitude, they follow routine paths as opposed to setting new operational procedures and methods (O'Brien 1983).

Developing country public-sector enterprises follow a similar pattern of market growth strategies. Most of them explore market growth opportunities within their core business system, with very few of them attempting to move away from their core business. As it is illustrated in Table 2, public-sector enterprises engage in market penetration, market development, and

TABLE 2. Market Growth Opportunity Matrix for Public Sector Enterprises in Overseas Markets.

| PRODUCT MARKET DOMAIN | | PRODUCTS/SERVICES OFFERED | |
|---|---|---|---|
| | | PRESENT PRODUCT/SERVICE | NEW PRODUCT/SERVICE |
| M A R K E T S   S E R V E D | P R E S E N T   M A R K E T S | 1. MARKET PENETRATION<br>• Increase sales regionally in domestic markets<br>• Increase sales nationally<br>• Concentrate efforts in backward sectors and industries<br>• Indirect exporting | 3. PRODUCT DEVELOPMENT<br>• Management contracting<br>• Turnkey projects<br>• Joint ventures<br>• Multinational marketing |
| | N E W   M A R K E T S | 2. MARKET DEVELOPMENT<br>• Direct exporting<br>• Countertrading<br>• Sub-contracting<br>• Foreign marketing<br>• Forming trading houses<br>• Leasing | 4. DIVERSIFICATION<br>• Involvement in financing and banking<br>• Vertical integration<br>• Direct foreign investment<br>• Product/service diversification of concentric, horizontal, and conglomerate type |

Source: The framework used was adapted from: H. Igor Ansoff, "Strategies for Diversification," *Harvard Business Review*, September-October 1957, pp. 113-124.

product/service development strategies while exploring growth opportunities in overseas markets. Only a very small proportion of developing-country public-sector enterprises diversify into numerous industries worldwide.

As part of its socio-economic and political restructuring, the People's Republic of China (PRC) has taken two major steps toward opening the country to wider foreign trade and investment. In the first instance, the PRC's National Chemicals Import and Export Corporation (Sinochem) go multinational as well as diversification. In General Manager, Zheng Dunxuns's words:

> Sinochem will explore new channels for the country to gain foreign currency. We will make efforts to promote economic efficiency and develop diverse operations, and eventually turn Sinochem into a new kind of socialist transnational corporation. (*Chemical & Engineering News* 1988, p. 4)

It is further stated that Sinochem will become a comprehensive economic entity, being responsible not only for imports and exports but also for production, finance, transportation, insurance, leasing, advertising, real estate, and services. The enterprise will also diversify into other oil and chemical-related businesses. Given the needed autonomy and flexibility, the public-sector enterprise can seek foreign funds, launch joint ventures and co-production agreements, and develop better trade and other forms of counter-trade. The public-sector enterprise can also process materials provided by customers, act as agent for others, and import and export chemical technology and equipment. In addition to these growth opportunities, Sinochem has moved into oil refining, set up a petroleum station in Singapore, and has plans to build filling stations in Europe. The enterprise has a shipping joint venture, and it expanded barter and entrepot trade in petroleum, chemical fertilizers, and plastics (*Chemical & Engineering News* 1988, p. 4).

### Global Competitiveness of PSEs

Over the past three decades, most developing-country governments have invested directly in productive activities through state-owned enterprises. Because of their rather poor performance domestically as well as internationally, a variety of developing countries as varied in size, history, and economic and political systems such as Argentina, China, Hungary, India, Morocco, Sudan, Togo, and Turkey have redefined the role of the state in productive economic activities as well as its role in the operational policies and strategies of public enterprises. For the improvement in the efficiency of public enterprises abroad, these enterprises are required to behave like autonomous profit-oriented businesses operating in a competitive environment. Developing-country governments should set clear business objectives, allowing market-determined investment, pricing, costs, and these governments should also allow a free market environment which helps in creating financial viability, ensuring management autonomy and accountability, selecting personnel based on business considerations, and establishing a performance-based reward system (Kohli and Sood 1987).

Recently, some public-sector enterprises have gained significant importance in international markets. Many firms from newly industrialized countries are now significant competitors in global markets for fairly technical non-labor intensive products and services. It is demonstrated by many researchers that foreign trade is the most important factor in promoting developing countries' economic growth and development (Aggarwal and Agmon 1990; Agmon and Kindleberger 1977; Aggarwal 1984; Lall 1984; Wells 1984; Linder 1986). For instance, the case of Brazilian-owned Petrobas (petroleum and related industries), Chilean-based Corporacion de Aceros del Pacifico (leading steel manufacturer in Latin America), Hindustan Machine Tools (large machine tool producers), Balmer Lawrie from India (barrels and cans), Taiwanese Fertilizers Company, and Guanomex from Mexico (fertilizers) are examples of successful public-sector enterprises worldwide. Their success, in most cases, depends on their organizational, strategic, and operational performance (Monkiewicz 1986, p. 69-70).

Which organizational structure a public-sector enterprise should adopt while operating in foreign markets depends much upon its past experience, maturity in international markets, and marketing strategies utilized. At the initial stage of international involvement, public enterprises create separate international departments to handle exports/foreign marketing. As products reach a stage of rapid growth in demand, marketing and production functions will develop. At an advanced stage of internationalization (multinational or transnational), product division has worldwide responsibility for production and marketing (Fingerhut and Hatano, 1983).

Public-sector enterprises either try to compete globally, or try to find niches in one or more national markets that are either geographically and/or culturally close to their domestic markets. Four broad alternatives are open to these enterprises.

- First, a public-sector enterprise can operate worldwide by competing in the full product line of its industry (or industries) using the advantages of a global operation. In most cases, implementation of this strategy necessitates a commitment of substantial resources and a long time horizon. This strategy is called *broad line global strategy.*

- The second strategy involves targeting a particular product line of the enterprise where impediments to global competition are low and the enterprise's position can be strong in a competitive global market. This strategy is called *global forces.*
- The third strategy calls for serving the particular needs of a national market(s) in order to out-compete global firms. This is termed *national focus strategy.*
- Finally, a strategy can be developed which can deal effectively in international markets where a number of government restrictions may hinder entry. This particular strategy is labeled *protected niche* (see Table 3).

Public-sector enterprises, especially those from developing countries, have recently become a powerful force in the international business scene. The example of Ethiopian Airlines can be cited as a case in point. The Ethiopian airlines have been made effective and profitable by introducing certain structural, organizational, and operational changes in its task and macro environments.

First, the airline has established good relations with its government. Second, it has kept up foreign contacts, and has used them wisely as a method of expanding. Third, it has taken a realistic view of its market, and has appreciated that regional markets in the developing world are better propositions than either a small and poor domestic market or an attempt to

TABLE 3. Public Enterprise Generic Strategies in International Markets

| | | COMPETITION AND OPERATIONS IN MARKETS | |
| --- | --- | --- | --- |
| | | WORLDWIDE | SPECIFIC MARKETS |
| P R O D U C T | B R O A D | (1)<br>Broad Line Global Strategy | (3)<br>National Focus |
| | N A R R O W | (2)<br>Global Focus | (4)<br>Protected Niche |

Source: Adapted from Michael E. Porter, *Comparative Strategy,* (New York: The Free Press, 1980), p. 294.

make it in the developed world, where it can be beaten up by big, rich carriers (*The Economist*, 1987 p. 86).

There has been a substantial policy change in international operations of public-sector enterprises from developing countries. There is a need for appropriate strategies for the development of successful public enterprises. Improved performance of these enterprises will contribute to socio-economic and technological development of developing countries where public-sector enterprises play a pivotal role.

## *CONCLUSIONS*

The most fundamental issue in the internationalization of public-sector enterprises from developing countries is the concern of how one can best identify alternative market-growth opportunities for improving effectiveness of domestic-country public-sector enterprises within the global marketplace. It is also important to understand micro relationships between public-sector enterprise production and marketing activities in the domestic market. Finally, exploration of the process of internationalization of public-sector enterprises in terms of international marketing implications is to be carried out. To this end, methods and procedures should be designed to facilitate international transactions of developing-country public-sector enterprise and coordinate product and service flows in the international marketing channels for major products, side by side products offered by private firms.

Public sector enterprises traditionally have utilized a monopoly concept in domestic markets. However, the expansion to global markets requires some significant strategy adjustments. In other words, customer orientation for the public sector enterprises means making radical changes in their corporate philosophy. First, it is necessary that these companies should adopt a business mentality (i.e., profit making units) and integration of a competitive approach into methods of work to avoid monopoly habits. Second, finding a niche or segment in international markets and evolution from uniformity to flexible range of services are vital for them. Finally, adopting a globalization objective instead of national objective as the long term policy for the corporation. A reform of the state enterprise structure should follow the example of Western European countries and Hungary by becoming self-managed and self-supporting units. Their manager should be chosen by and be more responsible to a board independent from the government with the remuneration of management being made dependent on the firm's profits. The application of market prices to the output and the inputs of state enterprises, and the rationalization of these prices through the adoption of realistic exchange rates and interest rates and, subsequently, the reform of the system of protection (Balassa 1981, p. 323-324). In another case, to improve performance and provide incentive for better managed public enterprises, Pakistan introduced a "signaling system." The system provides very clear and quantifiable performance targets for each public enterprise. An information system is developed for each enterprise, and domestic as well as international marketing performance is evaluated on a routine basis (Hartmann and Nawab 1985).

Furthermore, it is expected that developing country public sector enterprises to pass through several interconnected dynamic phases in their globalization process. Perhaps government assisted internationalization process could be employed more successfully than other programs. In other words, sequential stages in the globalization process include import substitution, export promotion, and foreign direct investment. It is expected that the effect of the government in the initial stages will be high while it diminishes in the later stages.

It may be proposed that public-sector enterprises from developing countries will continue to be more heavily export/foreign-marketing oriented in the late 90's and beyond. These enterprises should follow the export/foreign-marketing route. In particular, export of basic chemicals by public enterprises of oil producing countries will gain more importance. However, it would perhaps be more feasible to compete as a multinational or transnational enterprise, and formulate plans for overseas markets (Mazzolini 1980).

Although most international marketing activities of public-sector enterprises are home-country (Ethnocentric) oriented, one expects more joint international business ventures between public-sector enterprises and multinational corporations, as enterprise activities from the public and private sectors compliment each other in many ways. Another anticipated development may be that of a change away from the international marketing of raw materials, services, and semi-processed goods toward increased marketing of manufactured products. For this to be effective, a considerable degree of active involvement in international marketing and exploration of global market opportunities is a must. Furthermore, implementation of host-country-oriented marketing strategies will pave the way for effective enterprise performance worldwide.

## *SUGGESTIONS FOR FUTURE RESEARCH*

This study conceptually analyzed the involvement of the developing country public sector enterprises in the global markets. Future studies should empirically analyze, using secondary and primary data sources, the impact of the globalization on the business operations of the public sector enterprises at domestic markets. This could involve a comparative analysis between the globalized public sector enterprise management/marketing philosophy (i.e., marketing orientation) and domesticated public sector enterprise management/marketing philosophy.

Another important area of the study in this subject is the comparison of the marketing strategies of newly globalized public sector enterprises and the marketing strategies of the newly globalized private sector enterprises. It is also desirable to initiate an experimental study to identify the variables and assess their importance in increasing effectiveness of successful public sector enterprises.

## REFERENCES

Ackerman, Marc (1994), "Privatization of Public-Assembly-Facility Management," *The Cornell H.R.A. Quarterly*, April, 72-83.

Alexander, W. Robert J. (1994), "The Government Sector, The Export Sector and Growth," *De Economist* 142, 211-220.

Aggarwal, R. and T. Agmon, "The International Success of Developing Country Firms: Role of Government-Directed Comparative Advantage," *Management International Review*, Vol. 30, No. 2, 1990, 163-180.

Aggarwal, R., "The Strategic Challenge of Third World Multinationals: A New Stage of the Product Life Cycle of Multinationals," in *Advances in International Comparative Management*, eds., R. N. Farmer, 1984, 103-122.

Agmon, T. and C. P. Kindleberger, "*Multinationals from Small Countries*, Cambridge, MA: The MIT Press, 1977.

Balassa, B., *The Newly Industrializing Countries in the World Economy*, Pergamon Press, New York, 1981, 323-324.

Beveridge, Bretta (1995), "Marketing Needed in the Public Sector," *Marketing News*, January 2, p.34.

Bradran, M. and B. Hinings, "Strategies of Administrative Control and Contextual Constraints in a Less-Developed Country: The Case of Egyptian Public Enterprise," *Organization Studies*, Vol. 2, 1981, pp. 3-21.

Cavusgil, S.T. and J.R. Nevin, "A Conceptualization of the Initial Involvement in International Marketing," in *Theoretical Developments in Marketing* in C. W. Lamb and P. M. Dunne (eds.), Chicago: American Marketing Association, 1980, pp. 68-71.

Chemical and Engineering News, "China's Reforms: Chemical Firm to Go Multinational," Vol. 66, No. 6, February 8, 1988, pp. 4-5.

Connolly, S.G., "Joint Ventures with Third World Multinationals: A New Form of Entry to International Markets," *Columbia Journal of World Business*, Vol. 19, No. 2, Summer 1984, pp. 18-22.

Cornell, D., "Transferring the "People's Livelihood" to the People: An Evaluation of Taiwan's Privatization Drive," *Law and Policy in International Business*, 24(3), Spring 1993, 943-992.

Gillis, M. and I. Peprah, "State-Owned Enterprises in Developing Countries," *The Wharton Magazine*, Vol. 6, No. 2, Winter 1981-82, pp. 32-40.

Fingerhut, E.C. and D.G. Hatano, "Principles of Strategic Planning Applied to International Corporations," *Managerial Planning*, Vol. 32, No. 2, September-October 1983, pp. 4-14.

Hartmann, A. and S.A. Nawab, "Evaluating Public Manufacturing Enterprises in Pakistan," *Finance and Development*, Vol. 22, No. 3, September 1985, pp. 27-30.

Heenan, D.A., "Moscow Goes Multinational," *Harvard Business Review*, Vol. 59, No. 3, May-June 1981, pp. 48, 52, 54, 56 and 58.

Johansson, J.K. and J.E. Vahlne, "The Internationalization of the Firm: A Model of Knowledge Development and Increasing Foreign Commitments," *Journal of International Business Studies*, October 1975, pp. 305-322.

Jorgensen, J.J., T. Hafsi and M.N. Kiggundu, "Toward a Market Imperfections Theory of Organizational Structure in Developing Countries," *Journal of Management Studies*, Vol. 23, No. 4, July 1986, pp. 417-442.

Kaynak, E., *International Marketing Management*, Praeger Publishers Inc., New York, 1984.

Kohli, H.S. and A. Sood, "Fostering Enterprise Development," *Finance and Development*, Vol. 24, No. 1, March 1987, pp. 34-36.

Lall, S., *The New Multinationals: The Spread of the Third World Multinationals*, John Wiley, New York, 1984.

Linder, S. B., *The Pacific Century: Economic and Political Consequences of Asian-Pacific Dynamism*, Stanford, CA: Stanford University Press, 1986.

Mazzolini, R., "Government Policies and Government Controlled Enterprises," *Columbia Journal of World Business*, Vol. 15, No. 3, Fall 1980, pp. 47-54.

Menzies, H.D., "U.S. Companies in Unequal Combat, *Fortune*, April 9, 1979, pp. 102-106.

Monkiewicz, J., "Multinational Enterprises of Developing Countries," *Management International Review*, Vol. 26, No. 3, 1986, pp. 67-79.

Naidu, G. M. and T. R. Rao, "Public Sector Promotion of Exports" A Needs-Based Approach," *Journal of Business Research*, 27, 1993, 85-101.

Nielsen, H., "The Prevailing Danish Attitudes Towards Public Enterprises," in G. Sorensen and O. J. Sorensen (eds.) *State Enterprise: Development in Business as Usual*, Aalborg University Press, Aalborg, Denmark, 1982, pp. 179-229.

O'Brien, P., "Relations Between Transnational Corporations and Public Enterprises in Developing Countries with Particular Reference to Technological Development: A Preliminary Analysis, Vienna," July 1983.

Papathanassopoulos, S., "Public Service Broadcasting and Deregulatory Pressures in Europe," *Journal of Information Science*, 16, 1990, 113-120.

Premchand, A., "Government and Public Enterprises–The Budget Link," *Finance and Development*, Vol. 16, No. 4, December 1979, pp. 27-30.

Ramamurti, R., "Performance Evaluation of State-Owned Enterprises in Theory and Practice," *Management Science*, Vol. 33, No. 7, July 1987, pp. 876-893.

Rhodes, J.B., "Economic Growth and Government-Owned Multinationals," *Management Review*, Vol. 68, No. 2, February 1979, pp. 31-32.

Robinson, R.D., *International Business Management*, 2nd ed. (Hinsdale, Ill.: Dryden Press, 1978), pp. 657-658.

Schoo, E.M., "European Community's Trade Relations with Developing Countries," *World Economy*, Vol. 9, No. 3, September 1986, pp. 313-318.

Snavely, Keith (1991). "Marketing in the Government Sector: A Public Policy Model," *American Review of Public Administration*, Vol. 21 (4), 311-326.

Soldner, G.H., "Management Orientations and Basic Strategies in International Marketing," in P. Hammann and B. Tietz (eds.) *Sixth Annual Workshop on Research in Marketing*, Saarbruc ken, West Germany, April 13-15, 1977, pp. ix-21-26.

Terpstra V., *International Marketing*, 3rd ed. (Hinsdale, Ill.: Dryden Press, 1983).

*The Economist*, "The Qualities in Common," December 26, 1987, No. 305, pp. 86-87.

Treheux, M., "Privatization and Competition versus Public Service," *Telecommunications Policy*, December 1992, 16(9), 757-758.

Wells, L. T., *Third World Multinationals*, Cambridge, MA: The MIT Press, 1984.

White, E., "Joint Ventures of Public Enterprises in Argentina with Other Developing Countries," ICPE/UNCTAD, Ljubljano, 1983.

Wiechmann, U., "Integrating Multinational Marketing Activities," *Columbia Journal of World Business*, Winter 1974, pp. 7-16.

Zavialov, P.S. and G.G. Abramishvili, "Marketing in a Planned Socialist Economy," in J. Singh (ed.) *Marketing Strategy and the Developing World*, Institute of Marketing Management, New Delhi, 1982, pp. 199-208.

# Differences in Marketing Activities and Performance of Foreign and Domestic Manufacturing Firms in Nigeria

Sam C. Okoroafo

## INTRODUCTION

The environment under which business is conducted in many developing countries such as Nigeria has changed dramatically due to economic reforms (Bartlett 1990; Huszagh, Roxas & Keck 1992). Much of the changes involve liberalization of trade, investment, ownership, and monetary controls. Executives are thus presented with a more market oriented economy which differs from the previous government dominated system. Due to the new environment executives face, it would be interesting to determine whether appropriate marketing decisions are being made. It would be particularly interesting to compare the decisions/activities of domestic and foreign managers in Nigeria.

Sam C. Okoroafo is Associate Professor of Marketing and International Business at The University of Toledo, Toledo, OH. His research appeared in *Journal of Business Research, Management International Review, International Marketing Review, Journal of Economics and International Relations, Industrial Marketing Management*, and *Journal of Global Marketing*, among others.

The author wishes to acknowledge financial support from the Academic Challenge Fund of the Department of Management at The University of Toledo.

[Haworth co-indexing entry note]: "Differences in Marketing Activities and Performance of Foreign and Domestic Manufacturing Firms in Nigeria." Okoroafo, Sam C. Co-published simultaneously in the *Journal of Global Marketing* (International Business Press, an imprint of The Haworth Press, Inc.) Vol. 9, No. 4, 1996, pp. 109-118; and: *Marketing in the Third World* (ed: Denise M. Johnson, and Erdener Kaynak) International Business Press, an imprint of The Haworth Press, Inc., 1996, pp. 109-118. Single or multiple copies of this article are available from The Haworth Document Delivery Service [1-800-342-9678, 9:00 a.m. - 5:00 p.m. (EST). E-mail address: getinfo@haworth.com].

The purpose of this article is to determine how marketing activities and performance of foreign and domestic firms have varied in response to these environmental changes. It was assumed that environmental changes would cause firms to adopt new and different strategies in order to survive. Thus, this article examines the linkage between marketing activities and performance in a reforming economy.

Nigeria is one of forty-five countries that have implemented reform programs under the International Monetary Fund's structural adjustment program (SAP). Its economic reform initiatives such as floating of currencies, eliminating controls on trade, instituting investment incentives and privatizing state owned industries can only create a more market oriented and competitive environment (Okoroafo and Russow 1993). Nigeria's program is so radical that the chief executive officer of its largest company–United African Company, Mr. Shonekan referred to the changes as a "quiet revolution" (*Business Times* 1991).

## *LITERATURE REVIEW*

Marketing strategy is a key aspect of a firm's business strategy (Aaker 1988). A marketing strategy is typically designed around decisions dealing with product, price, distribution and promotional issues (McCarthy & Perreault 1993). Its objective is to satisfy customer needs. Customer need satisfaction occurs when all elements of the marketing system (i.e., suppliers, distributors) are working together. It is expected that a properly executed marketing strategy will enable firms achieve their typical objectives of increased sales, market share, and competitiveness.

Marketing activities are environment dependent (Huszagh, Huszagh & Hanks 1992). It was not long ago that the environments in developing countries were highly controlled. They were characterized by poor infrastructure, high trade barriers, high political risk and changing laws (Levis 1979; Elsaid & El-Hennawi 1982). These conditions have been well documented in many studies (e.g., Todaro 1989). Such conditions called for minimal performance of marketing activities. For instance, prices for products would be set based on government edicts (Tibesar and White 1989); products made and sold irrespective of mis-matches with consumer needs (Austin 1990); and promotional efforts underemphasized. Under a controlled environment foreign firms would be at a disadvantage relative to domestic firms. For instance, Baliga (1984) noted that executives from developed countries faced difficulty obtaining timely and accurate information on economic, political, and social conditions in developing countries.

It would be enlightening to determine strategies of firms in environments that have been evolving towards market control. Marketing activities are generally organized around the 4 Ps—promotion, place, product and price (Kotler 1991). Promotion enables firms to communicate the availability and merits of their products to customers. Product activities are designed to satisfy customer needs. "Place" activities aim to get the product to the customer at the appropriate place and time. Pricing activities is to ensure that customers value for products are properly identified and reflected. In addition, marketers work with suppliers and distributors to satisfy customers. These activities form the basis of the items used in this study. Chong (1973) used similar measures to compare the marketing practices of foreign and domestic firms in Malaysia and noted differences in marketing practices and profitability indicators.

In distinguishing between the marketing strategies of foreign and domestic firms, reference was made to the postulated behavior of the two groups from previous research. It was expected that foreign firms would pursue more market oriented strategies than domestic firms. For instance, foreign firms would emphasize customer service, and offer better product and quality package. They have products with recognizable brand names and pursue practices tested and perfected in their home markets. Foreign firms are familiar with competitive marketing activities because of their experience in their home markets. However, there is some evidence that local firms from some developing countries can compete effectively in foreign markets. For instance, Vachani (1989) showed that manufacturers of low-priced "crude" products have become effective competitors in some developing countries. In fact, they have managed to steal market share from some of the largest multinationals (e.g., Unilevel PLC).

Dadzie et al. (1988) looked at performance of marketing functions in five African markets and reported higher incidence and performance of market activities in a buyer's market situation rather than a seller's market. In general, the marketing concept in Nigeria has been accepted, but not practiced (Mitchell and Agenmonmon 1984). So, as the environment shifts from one where sellers are dominant to one where consumers enjoy greater freedoms, marketing activities become more important.

## RESEARCH METHOD

In order to determine changes in marketing strategy and performance, a survey of chief executives of top foreign and domestic manufacturing firms in Nigeria was conducted. Foreign companies which represented 36.5% of the sample had their headquarters in United Kingdom, France, South Korea, Norway, United States of America, Netherlands, Switzerland, Germany, and Sweden. The majority of firms (56.2%) had annual sales and assets greater than $4 million. A foreign firm was defined as one that has some percentage ownership from abroad.

The questionnaire asked for perceptions of how the economic reform programs have affected their marketing decisions and market performance. The strategy section had the statement, "My firm has adjusted its structure and strategy in response to SAP by. . . ." followed by the items listed in Table 1. The performance section had the statement, "In my view, SAP has resulted in an increase in my firm's. . . ." followed by the items in Table 3. These information were collected using a five point Likert scale (5 = strongly agree to 1 = strongly disagree) (see Tables 2 & 4). Also, the

TABLE 1. Comparison of Marketing Strategy*

| Variables | Domestic Companies? | | Foreign Companies** | |
|---|---|---|---|---|
| | Mean | Std. Dev. | Mean | Std. Dev. |
| streamlining subsidiaries | 3.094 | 1.146 | 2.870 | 1.014 |
| reducing number of employees | 3.568 | 1.191 | 3.346 | .977 |
| increasing R&D expenditures | 3.306 | 1.167 | 3.280 | .843 |
| new product introduction | 3.405 | 1.040 | 3.803 | .801 |
| product improvement | 3.730 | .932 | 3.880 | .927 |
| local sourcing | 3.838 | 1.214 | 3.577 | .987 |
| emphasize strategic planning | 3.974 | 1.000 | 4.038 | .774 |
| increased promotion | 3.676 | 1.002 | 3.885 | .816 |
| competitive pricing | 3.895 | .894 | 3.962 | .916 |
| control over distributors | 2.811 | .995 | 3.038 | .871 |
| demanding better service from suppliers | 3.605 | .974 | 3.962 | .774 |
| better customer service | 3.632 | 1.101 | 4.038 | .871 |
| improved manufacturing process | 3.432 | 1.144 | 3.654 | .892 |
| opening up new branches | 2.861 | .961 | 2.577 | .987 |
| foreign market diversification | 3.200 | 1.052 | 2.846 | 1.047 |
| increased remittance to HQ | 2.353 | .917 | 2.560 | 1.044 |
| transfer price at above market price | 2.387 | .919 | 2.208 | .721 |
| re-investment | 3.405 | 1.279 | 3.385 | .898 |

* Results based on perceptions
? N = 54
** N = 31
Scale: 1 = low and 5 = high

TABLE 2. Comparison of Importance of Marketing Strategy Variables*

| Variables | Domestic Companies? | | Foreign Companies** | |
|---|---|---|---|---|
| | Mean | Std. Dev. | Mean | Std. Dev. |
| streamlining subsidiaries | 2.697 | .847 | 2.400 | 1.225 |
| reducing number of employees | 2.711 | .898 | 3.000 | .980 |
| increasing R&D expenditures | 2.811 | .877 | 2.577 | .902 |
| new product introduction | 3.865 | .751 | 3.192 | .981 |
| product improvement | 3.189 | .660 | 3.154 | .967 |
| local sourcing | 3.243 | .683 | 3.269 | .962 |
| emphasize strategic planning | 3.368 | .675 | 3.231 | .992 |
| increased promotion | 3.027 | .687 | 3.308 | .884 |
| competitive pricing | 3.237 | .714 | 3.346 | .936 |
| control over distributors | 2.865 | .713 | 2.885 | .864 |
| demanding better service from supplier | 2.892 | .737 | 3.346 | .797 |
| better customer service | 3.053 | .899 | 3.231 | .863 |
| improved manufacturing process | 2.944 | .715 | 3.000 | 1.000 |
| opening up new branches | 2.778 | .722 | 2.692 | 1.192 |
| foreign market diversification | 2.778 | .722 | 2.720 | 1.242 |
| increased remittance to HQ | 2.788 | .781 | 3.000 | 1.233 |
| transfer price at above market price | 2.606 | .781 | 2.538 | 1.363 |
| re-investment | 2.972 | .654 | 3.000 | .894 |

\*   Results based on perceptions
?   N = 54
\*\*  N = 31
!   Scale: 1 = low to 5 = high

level of importance of each factor to firms' success was measured using another five point scale (1 = low to 5 = high). The variables used to measure marketing performance were sales, market share, ability to gain market share, sales growth rate, return on investment, profits and competitive position. According to Burke (1984) and Douglas and Craig (1983), these are adequate measures for marketing activities. Respondents were asked not to assign any weights if they perceived all factors equal in importance. Finally, information on the characteristics of the respondent firms was obtained.

Subjects of the study consisted of the managing directors of 200 manufacturing firms in Nigeria. Their names and addresses were obtained from "Redasel's Companies of Nigeria" (1988). Companies were chosen based on reported minimum sales ($2 million), assets ($4 million), and employees (300). The objective was to select the largest manufacturing

TABLE 3. Comparison of Firm Performance*

| | Domestic Companies? | | Foreign Companies** | |
|---|---|---|---|---|
| Variables | Mean | Std. Dev. | Mean | Std. Dev. |
| sales | 2.895 | 1.331 | 3.077 | 1.197 |
| market share | 3.139 | 1.046 | 2.846 | 1.047 |
| ability to gain mkt share | 3.216 | 1.031 | 3.115 | .952 |
| sales growth rate | 2.944 | .984 | 2.923 | .977 |
| return on investment | 2.459 | 1.016 | 2.577 | .945 |
| profits | 2.784 | 1.109 | 2.808 | 1.021 |
| competitive position | 3.432 | .899 | 3.192 | 1.096 |

\* Results based on perceptions
? N = 54
\*\* N = 31
Scale: 1 = low and 5 = high

TABLE 4. Comparison of Importance of Performance Variables*

| | Domestic Companies? | | Foreign Companies** | |
|---|---|---|---|---|
| Variables | Mean | Std. Dev. | Mean | Std. Dev. |
| sales | 3.368 | .714 | 3.846 | .834 |
| market share | 3.135 | .631 | 3.600 | .816 |
| ability to gain market share | 3.027 | .552 | 3.520 | .918 |
| sales growth rate | 3.079 | .587 | 3.654 | .846 |
| return on investment | 3.054 | .780 | 3.346 | .977 |
| profits | 3.081 | .862 | 3.615 | .983 |
| competitive position | 2.946 | .575 | 3.654 | .892 |

\* Results based on perceptions
? N = 54
\*\* N = 31
Scale: 1 = low and 5 = high

firms. The respondent list generated was highly correlated to a listing of "top 100 industrial companies" found in another publication–*ThisWeek* (1989).

Following a pretest, two mailings were done. The follow-up was sent two months later to 100 nonrespondents to ascertain if their responses were significantly different from those who had responded initially. Sixty (60) and twenty-five (25) responses were received from the initial and follow-up mailings respectively.

Of the eighty-five (85) total responses, eighty-one (81) were usable resulting in an effective response rate of forty (40.5) percent. This response rate is significantly better than those for this type of audience. For instance, Mitchell and Agenmonmen (1984) sent 200 questionnaires to business executives in Nigeria and obtained a 32.5% response rate. The high response rate is attributed to the significance and timing of the study as well as publicity generated during collection through press interviews. In fact, eighty (80) percent of respondents requested copies of the results.

## RESULTS

The mean scores on marketing activities and performance variables as well as the perceived importance of those items were used to draw conclusions. All means were significant at the .005 level. To interpret the results, items with a mean score greater than 3 reflect performance of an activity while items with less than 3 indicate non-performance. The standard deviation indicates the degree of consensus around the mean.

### Comparison of Marketing Strategy

When differences in all marketing activities were compared, no significant differences were found. However, an item by item analysis revealed some interesting findings (Table 1). Domestic firms were more likely to streamline subsidiaries, reduce the number of employers, and increase research and development expenditure. The emphasis on cost cutting measures by domestic firms can be explained since those firms would have been more inefficient in a controlled market environment. Also, the increased emphasis on research and development may reflect a renewed effort to be technologically up to date. It is however surprising that domestic firms are seeking to diversify into foreign markets following the strategy of Indian firms as reported in Vachani (1989).

As expected foreign firms seemed to greatly emphasize marketing activities such as strategic planning, promotion, competitive pricing and control over distributors. Particular note should be made of strategy emphasis in the customer service area. Not only do foreign firms emphasize customer service, they demand better service from their suppliers.

### Importance of Marketing Activities

In determining the importance of marketing variables, it was noted that foreign firms considered promotion, pricing, and customer service more important than domestic firms. However, domestic firms thought new product introduction more critical. To the extent that domestic firms consider marketing decisions (i.e., promotion, pricing, customer service) of less importance, this may affect their competitiveness in the future.

### *Comparison of Performance*

The results show low market performance by both domestic and foreign firms. Foreign firms are happier with their sales performance. However, by most other measures of performance–market share, ability to gain market share, and competitive position, domestic firms seem to be doing better. This can be explained since guarantees and preferences were received by domestic firms under protective environments. It would take some time for such advantages to disappear. It would be interesting to find out whether such advantages will be maintained over time. Particular note should be made of the low profits being incurred by both domestic and foreign firms. This is expected due to introduction of expensive market adjustment programs.

### *Importance of Performance Measures*

This measure provides an indication of the marketing objectives firms would pursue or emphasize. Overwhelmingly, foreign firms perceive all these measures of marketing performance more significant than domestic firms. Thus, it seems that they would continue to structure their activities to increase sales, market share and competitive position.

## *CONCLUSION*

This study has identified differences in marketing activities and performance of domestic and foreign firms in Nigeria. The finding suggests that foreign firms are practicing those marketing activities necessary to survive in an increasingly competitive environment. This spells long term concerns for domestic firms that would need to stay competitive to survive. The results may be due to ignorance of the significance of marketing activities on the part of domestic firms. Educating managers on the role of marketing in enhancing firm performance is one solution to this issue. Another finding is that domestic firms were performing better than foreign firms in terms of market share, competitive position and ability to gain market share. However, foreign firms recognize the significance of these measures. This initial advantage may erode over time.

Although this study used firms in Nigeria only, it is still generalizable to other developing countries. It is not surprising then that Sadri and Williamson (1989) have stated that Nigeria is a good barometer for other developing countries.

## *LIMITATIONS*

The use of perceptual data could result in bias to the extent that it does not match up with actual data. However, the difficulty of obtaining actual data precludes any post research comparisons. Also, the cross sectional nature of the study is a weakness. However, limitations in time and financial resources necessitate its use.

## REFERENCES

Aaker, David (1988) *Developing Business Strategies*, 2nd ed, John Wiley Press, New York.

Austin, James E. (1990), *Managing in Developing Countries: Strategic Analysis and Operating Techniques*. The Free Press, New York.

Baliga, B.R. (1984), "World-views and Multinational Corporations' Investments in the Less Developed Countries" *Columbia Journal of World Business*, (Summer), p. 80-84.

Bartlett, Bruce, (1990), "Capitalism in Africa," *Journal of Developing Areas*, Vol 34, No. 3 (April), pp. 327-349.

Burke, Marian C. (1984), "Strategic Choice and Marketing Managers: An Examination of Business Level Marketing Objectives," *Journal of Marketing Research*, Vol. 21, (November), pp. 345-359.

*Business Times* (1991), "Challenges for Nigerian Industries," Vol 16, No. 3, Daily Times of Nigeria, PLC, Lagos, Nigeria, (Jan 21), p. 22

Chong, S. (1973), "Comparative Marketing Practices of Foreign and Domestic Firms in Developing Countries: A Case Study of Malaysia," *Management International Review*, Vol. 13, No. 6, pp. 91-98.

Dadzie, K.Q., I.P. Akaah, and E.A. Riordan (1988), "Incidence of Market Typologies and Pattern of Marketing Activity Performance in Selected African Countries" *Journal of Global Marketing*, Vol. 1, No. 3 (Spring), pp. 87-107.

Douglas, S.P. and C.S. Craig (1983), "Examining Performance of U.S.Multinationals in Foreign Markets," *Journal of International Business Studies*, Vol. 16, No. 3, pp. 51-63.

Elsaid, H.H. and M.S. El-Hennawi (1982), "Foreign Direct Investments in LDCs: Egypt" *California Management Review*, Vol. 24, No. 4, (Summer), pp. 85-92.

Huszagh, S.M., J.P. Roxas, and K.L. Keck (1992), "Marketing Practices in the Changing Philippine Macroeconomic Environment," *International Marketing Review*, Vol. 9, 32-43.

Huszagh, S.M., F.W. Huszagh, and G.F. Hanks (1992), "Macroeconomic Conditions and International Marketing Management" *International Marketing Review*, Vol. 9, pp. 6-18.

Kotler, P. (1991), *Marketing Management: Analysis, Planning, and Control*. 7th ed., Prentice-Hall International, London.

Levis, M., (1979), "Does Political Instability in Developing Countries Affect Foreign Investment Flow? An Empirical Examination," *Management International Review*, Vol. 19, pp. 59-68.

McCarthy, J.E. and W. Perreault (1993), *Basic Marketing*, 11th edition, Homewood, IL: Irwin.

Mitchell, Ivor S. and Anthony I. Agenmonmen (1984), "Marketers' Attitudes Toward the Marketing Concept in Nigerian Business and Non-business Operations" *Columbia Journal of World Business*, Vol. 19, No. 3, (Fall), pp. 62-71.

Okoroafo, Sam and Lloyd Russow (1993), "Impact of Marketing Strategy on Performance: Empirical Evidence from a Liberalized Developing Country" *International Marketing Review*, vol. 10, No. 4-18.

*Redasel's Companies of Nigeria* (1988), 1st ed., Redasel's Research & Data Services Ltd, Lagos, Nigeria.

Sadri, Sorab and Caroline Williamson (1989), "Management and Industrial Relations Strategies of Multinational Corporations in Developing Countries" *Journal of Business Research*, Vol. 18, No. 3, (May), pp. 179-193.

*ThisWeek* (1989), *"Nigeria: The Top 100 Companies,"* No. 139, Published by ThisWeek Ltd, Lagos, Nigeria.

Tibesar, A. and R. White (1990), "Pricing Policy and Household Energy Use in Dakar, Senegal," *Journal of Developing Areas*, Vol. 25, No. 1, (October), pp. 33-48.

Todaro (1989), *Economic Development in the Third World*, 4th Edition, Longmans Publishers, New York.

Vachani, S. (1989), "Strategic Responses of Multinationals to Competition from Developing Country Cottage Firms," *International Marketing Review*, Vol. 7, No. 3, pp. 31-47.

# Index

Advertising
   of automobiles, 80,87n.
   relationship to economic
      development, 85-86
   on television
      for children, 83
      Indonesian ban on, 81
      in Papua New Guinea, 81,82
Agriculture
   as public-sector enterprise, 90
   as underdeveloped countries'
      economic base, 7
Airlines, as public-sector enterprise,
   90
American multinational
      corporations, foreign
      market-oriented marketing
      adaptations of, 57-74
   of consumer versus industrial
      products, 60,64,71
   distribution elements, 59,68-69
   by large versus small markets, 60
   pricing elements, 59,69,70-71
   product elements,
      59,61,62-64,65,
      66,67,69,70-71
   promotion elements, 59,63,65,
      67-68,69,70
   reasons for, 71
Amway, 68,69
Arby's, 69
Argentina
   multinational corporations'
      marketing adaptations in,
      61
   public-sector enterprises in, 101
   public-sector foreign ventures in,
      99

Automobile industry, as
      public-sector enterprise,
      90,91
Automobiles, advertising of, 80,87n.

Balmer Lawrie, 102
Bangladesh, public-sector enterprises
   in, 90
Bauxite industry, as public-sector
      enterprise, 90
*Best 1000 Corporations in the*
      *Philippines* (Mahal Kong
      Pilipinas Foundation), 16
Bolivia, public-sector-related Gross
      Domestic Product in, 90
Brand names
   globalization of, 62-64
   in South American markets,
      62-64,65,66,71
Brazil
   Amway in, 68
   multinational corporations'
      marketing adaptations in,
      58,65,66,68-70
   newspapers in, 67
   public-sector enterprises in, 90,
      95,102
Broad line global strategy, 102,103

Canadian manufacturing firms,
      product adaptation by, 39
Cartels, in wholesaling, 68
Chiclets chewing gum, 62
Children, television advertising for,
   83
Chile, public-sector enterprises in,
   102

   *119*

# Haworth
# DOCUMENT DELIVERY
# SERVICE

This valuable service provides a single-article order form for any article from a Haworth journal.

- *Time Saving:* No running around from library to library to find a specific article.
- *Cost Effective:* All costs are kept down to a minimum.
- *Fast Delivery:* Choose from several options, including same-day FAX.
- *No Copyright Hassles:* You will be supplied by the original publisher.
- *Easy Payment:* Choose from several easy payment methods.

*Open Accounts Welcome for . . .*
- Library Interlibrary Loan Departments
- Library Network/Consortia Wishing to Provide Single-Article Services
- Indexing/Abstracting Services with Single Article Provision Services
- Document Provision Brokers and Freelance Information Service Providers

**MAIL or *FAX* THIS ENTIRE ORDER FORM TO:**

Haworth Document Delivery Service
The Haworth Press, Inc.
10 Alice Street
Binghamton, NY 13904-1580

**or FAX:** 1-800-895-0582
**or CALL:** 1-800-342-9678
9am-5pm EST

PLEASE SEND ME PHOTOCOPIES OF THE FOLLOWING SINGLE ARTICLES:
1) Journal Title: _____
   Vol/Issue/Year: _____ Starting & Ending Pages: _____
   Article Title: _____
   _____

2) Journal Title: _____
   Vol/Issue/Year: _____ Starting & Ending Pages: _____
   Article Title: _____
   _____

3) Journal Title: _____
   Vol/Issue/Year: _____ Starting & Ending Pages: _____
   Article Title: _____
   _____

4) Journal Title: _____
   Vol/Issue/Year: _____ Starting & Ending Pages: _____
   Article Title: _____
   _____

**(See other side for Costs and Payment Information)**

*COSTS:* Please figure your cost to order quality copies of an article.

1. Set-up charge per article: $8.00

           ($8.00 × number of separate articles)      _____

2. Photocopying charge for each article:

                   1-10 pages: $1.00      _____

                   11-19 pages: $3.00      _____

                   20-29 pages: $5.00      _____

                   30+ pages: $2.00/10 pages      _____

3. Flexicover (optional): $2.00/article      _____

4. Postage & Handling: US: $1.00 for the first article/

                   $.50 each additional article      _____

                   Federal Express: $25.00      _____

                   Outside US: $2.00 for first article/

                   $.50 each additional article _____

5. Same-day FAX service: $.35 per page      _____

                  **GRAND TOTAL:** _____

---

*METHOD OF PAYMENT:* (please check one)

❑ Check enclosed    ❑ Please ship and bill. PO # _____

             (sorry we can ship and bill to bookstores only! All others must pre-pay)

❑ Charge to my credit card: ❑ Visa; ❑ MasterCard; ❑ Discover;

                ❑ American Express;

Account Number: _____ Expiration date: _____

Signature: ✗ _____

Name: _____ Institution: _____

Address: _____

_____

City: _____ State: _____ Zip: _____

Phone Number: _____ FAX Number: _____

---

## MAIL or *FAX* THIS ENTIRE ORDER FORM TO:

| | |
|---|---|
| Haworth Document Delivery Service | **or FAX:** 1-800-895-0582 |
| The Haworth Press, Inc. | **or CALL:** 1-800-342-9678 |
| 10 Alice Street | 9am-5pm EST) |
| Binghamton, NY 13904-1580 | |